SOLIDARITY WITH THE PEOPLE OF NICARAGUA

James McGinnis

ORBIS BOOKS
Maryknoll, New York 10545

Second Printing, July 1985

The Catholic Foreign Mission Society of America (Maryknoll) recruits and trains people for overseas missionary service. Through Orbis Books Maryknoll aims to foster the international dialogue that is essential to mission. The books published, however, reflect the opinion of their authors and are not meant to represent the official position of the society.

Copyright © 1985 by James McGinnis
All rights reserved
Manufactured in the United States of America

Manuscript Editor: William E. Jerman

Library of Congress Cataloging in Publication Data
McGinnis, James.
   Solidarity with the people of Nicaragua.

   Bibliography: p.
   1. Church and social problems—Nicaragua—Catholic Church. 2. Nicaragua—Social conditions—1979
I. Title.
HN39.N5M38 1985   282′.7285   84-27202
ISBN 0-88344-448-8 (pbk.)

SOLIDARITY WITH THE PEOPLE OF NICARAGUA

HONDURAS
Rio Coco
Jalapa
Ocotal
Siuna
Waslala
Esteli
Matagalpa
ZELAYA
Chinandega
Leon
Lake Managua
Masaya
Managua
Granada
Diriamba
Jinotepe
Bluefields
Lake Nicaragua
PACIFIC OCEAN
Solentiname
SanCarlos
CARIBBEAN SEA
COSTA RICA
Central America
= 50 miles
NICARAGUA

This book is the story of a people. Individual persons, yes, but even more fundamentally it is the story of "the people." It is the story of communities—local communities and national communities. And this book is addressed to a people. Individual persons, yes, but especially to communities—school groups, family groups, churches, and to "the people" of the United States and Canada.

Pueblo al Pueblo—People to People

El pueblo—the people
El pueblo nicaragüense,
a people united as a nation,
determined to determine itself,
a people that has struggled and died
and in that struggle continues to forge itself
as a people—*el pueblo.*

2 1/2 million persons celebrating
their fifth anniversary
by fighting for that freedom
against the most powerful
military and economic force in the world,
a government supposedly "of the people,
for the people, by the people."

El pueblo nicaragüense—
Clarisa at 22, Maura the grandmother,
Silvio the prisoner,
Jorge his Sandinista *jefe*—
their lives are the story
of the "new Nicaragua";
a people willing, wanting, to embrace
us as equals,
as Lupita embraced us
with a kiss of peace
on the anniversary of the death
of her sons, children fighting a dictator
and killed by weapons supplied
by our government.

But that government is not
"the people," they say.
How do "the people" feel? they ask.

How do we, the people, feel?
How do we the people respond to this invitation
from *"el pueblo nicaragüense"?*

Contents

Acknowledgments xi
Acronyms xiii
Introduction 1

Chapter One
U.S. Policy toward Nicaragua 5
  Historical Overview   5
  Current U.S. Policy   7
      The U.S. and Nicaragua, April 1982   7
    Analysis of the U.S. Policy Statement   10
    Escalation of U.S. Hostility   18
      The Contadora Peace Process   18
      Invasion of Grenada   19
      Kissinger Commission Report   19
      Military Escalation in Honduras   20
      Mining of Nicaraguan Ports   22
  An Alternative Policy   22
      The Blueprint in Brief   23

Chapter Two
Ciudad Sandino and St. Louis:
A Solidarity Pairing Project 26
  The Revolution in a Barrio Context   26
    Religion   28
    Health Care Services   28
    Maura Otero   33
    A Mental Health Team   35
    Literacy Campaign   36
    Maryknoll in Ciudad Sandino   38
  The Pairing   39
  Further Dimensions of Pairing   47

Chapter Three
Nicaraguan Christian Youth Groups:
Youth Pairing Project Possibilities   50
    Barrio Monseñor Lezcano Youth Group   50
        Clarisa   *51*
        Estrella   *54*
    La Merced Youth Group   56
    The Nicaraguan Government and the Catholic Hierarchy   60
    An Ecumenical Christian Youth Movement   63
    Revolutionary-Christian Youth Leaders   64
        Emanuel Martínez G.   *64*
        Walter Samuel Diaz N.   *65*
        Sergio Rivas P.   *65*
        Javier Torres B.   *66*
        Orlando Pérez V.   *66*
    The MJCI and Christian Unity   67
    Appendix   69

Chapter Four
Witness for Peace:
Solidarity Political Action   72
    Jalapa   74
        Nonviolent Presence   *74*
        Standing with the People   *75*
        Praying with the People   *78*
        Working with the People   *79*
        Nonviolent Protest   *80*
            The Attack on the Town of Waslala   82
    WFP Projects in the U.S.A.   87
            A Pledge of Resistance   87

Chapter Five
Children's Solidarity Projects   95
    "Solidarity Parks" for Jalapa   95
    Pairing and Pen Pals   99
    "Playgrounds, Not Battlegrounds"   99
    Community Development in León   102
    Other Projects   105

CONTENTS ix

    Youth Center in Jalapa   105
    Early Childhood Program near Ocotal   105
    Child Care Center in Ocotal   106

Chapter Six
Nicaraguan Coffee:
A Solidarity Buying Project   **108**
    Economic Analysis and Our Response   109
        The Third World: Resource-rich, Dollar-poor   109
        Coffee as an Example of Inequities in World Trade   111
        An Alternative Trading System   114
        Buying Nicaraguan Coffee from Friends
            of the Third World   115
    Nicaraguan Coffee—and Nicaraguans   117

Chapter Seven
Other Solidarity Projects   **124**
    La Granja   124
        Nicaraguan Prison Policies   124
        Letting Dignity Work   127
        How to Help   131
    Medical Aid for Nicaragua   131
    AFSC Nicaragua Appeal   136
    Tools for Peace   136
    Humanitarian Aid for Nicaraguan Democracy   136
    Work Brigades for Nicaragua   137
    People-Pants and Spare Parts   137
    Pueblo-to-People   138
    MADRE   139
    Fr. Bernie Survil   141
    Central America Peace Campaign:
        "Talks, Not Troops"   142

Chapter Eight
The Inner Core of Solidarity   **144**
    Side-by-Side Service   144
    Simplifying Our Lifestyles   145
    Prayer   149
    Fasting   153

A Call to Prayer   154
A Way of Expressing Our Dependence on God   154
An Instrument of Discipleship   155
A Means of Solidarity   155
An Invitation to Service   156
Fasting and Prayer with Others   156

Resources   **157**
Groups/Projects Described in This Book   157
Audiovisual and Printed Materials   159
Audiovisuals   159
Books   160
Periodicals and Pamphlets   161

Acknowledgments

This book is partially an effort to say thank you to the persons whose lives are told in its pages—lives that offer so much hope and inspiration. Special gratitude is due to our hosts in Nicaragua —to Mary Hartman in Managua; to Peggy Healy, Bea Zaragoza, and the other Maryknoll sisters and lay missioners; and to the people of Jalapa for my second journey to Nicaragua. My sister Mary Anne was an invaluable asset as translator, guide, and companion on the first journey. My wife, Kathy, our son Tom, and I wish also to thank Maryknoll Fathers Tom Marti and Dan Driscoll, and the entire Maryknoll community in New York, for opening up to us their Latin American network of dedicated missioners. They have, in turn, helped to open up our lives even more to God's dynamic presence in the world through the struggle of the people of God for justice. Angie O'Gorman, Jim and Nanette Ford, and my wife, Kathy, all made many helpful suggestions on the original text. Brother Camillus Dufresne, Mary Hartman, Bea Zaragoza, and especially Celine Woznica and Anne Rodman contributed significantly to its revision. Yvonne Dilling (Witness for Peace) and Sax Sperry (Friends of the Third World) provided part of the data for chapters 4 and 6. Lucky Hollander, Maura Nagle Peterson, and Barbara Ginter, CSJ, helped considerably with chapter 5. Leroy and Ruth Zimmerman, Diana and Jim Oleskovich, Mark and Kate Robinson, Sue and Ron Williams, and Jim and Peggy Herning all contributed their reflections to chapter 2.

Finally, I am grateful to John Eagleson and the staff of Orbis Books for their support, both of the original book and project, and especially of this amplified revision. One of the reasons for their willingness to publish the book is their shared realization that the situation in Nicaragua is urgent and every solidarity action, especially those with public education and political action possibilities, can make a difference. At stake in Central America are not only the lives of millions of persons but also the very soul of the United States of America. Thus, it is for our own sake as a people and nation, as well as for the sake of the people of Nicaragua, that we each need to do whatever it is we can to address U.S. policy there and to stand with our sisters and brothers on the receiving end of this policy.

Acronyms

AFSC	American Friends Service Committee
ANS	Sandinista Children's Association
CAV	Antonio Valdivieso (Ecumenical) Center
CDS	Sandinista Defense Committee
CEP	Popular Education Collective
CEPAD	Evangelical Committee for Aid and Development
CONFER	Conference of Religious
ECR	Revolutionary Christian Students
FSLN	Sandinista National Liberation Front
HAND	Humanitarian Aid for Nicaraguan Democracy
ICO	International Coffee Organization
INPRHU	Institute of Human Promotion
MINVAH	Ministry of Housing
MJCI	Interdenominational Christian Youth Movement
NACLA	North American Congress on Latin America
NNSNP	National Network of Solidarity with the Nicaraguan People
OPEN	Permanent National Emergency Operation
ORD	Organization of Disabled Revolutionaries
PACCA	Policy Alternatives for the Caribbean and Central America
RS	*Responsable de salud*
UNAN	National Autonomous University of Nicaragua
UNEN	Student Union of Nicaragua
WFP	Witness for Peace

Introduction

This book and the whole project from which it emerged focus on a fundamental human/religious reality—that we are one global family. Many of us lack concrete experience or realization of this fact. It has not as yet become a reality in our hearts and in our daily actions. One way to make this theoretical truth a practical reality in our lives is by linking ourselves and also our family, our youth or school group, our church or social action committee, with a specific group of persons in another part of the world. As Robert McAfee Brown puts it:

> Visions alone are not enough. In addition to ecumenical vision, we need a second thing, which we might call ecumenism as energizer. There must not only be a vision of the global family, but a sufficient sense of belonging to the global family so people will undertake risks on behalf of that broad family.

Individuals will frequently take risks for their immediate families or for the family sometimes called the nation. They can be so energized because they believe in the reality of their vision. Once again, the hopeful thing about the global family is that it does exist.

On occasion we meet, or become intensely aware of, a brother or sister from Chile or the Philippines or South Korea or Thailand or Brazil. These countries are only a few of the places in which our parochial community, the nation, oppresses those who are our brothers and sisters in the ecumenical community.

We are not left merely with an "ideal," in other words; the ecumenical community has enough flesh and blood reality so we can occasionally make true commitments to those

2   INTRODUCTION

who live within it ["Ecumenism-Solidarity," *National Catholic Reporter*, April 8, 1977].

This book is the story of one group of brothers and sisters—the people of Nicaragua—and specific ways we can link our lives with them in a common pursuit of shalom—of peace, justice, integrity, and unity. As the U.S. government tries to oppress them and overturn their Revolution, the people of North America and elsewhere can respond in solidarity with the people of Nicaragua. This response is basically twofold. In the face of the destructiveness of U.S. policy, it is a resounding no that expresses itself in political action challenging that policy—political action ranging from the more traditional forms of public education, letter-writing, and the like, to more dramatic and risky forms of nonviolent witness and direct action. In the face of the constructiveness of Nicaraguan efforts to build a new society embodying much of the biblical concept of shalom, our response is an empowering yes that can express itself in a variety of material or financial support projects, in "pairing" and several forms of on-site solidarity work, and also in symbolic and spiritual ways.

This book does not describe every Nicaraguan solidarity project and group, and does not exhaust the variety of individual and collective responses to any social issue, but it does describe most of the major, current U.S. Nicaraguan solidarity projects and tries to articulate the basic elements of an "integrated" response. On the level of what some call the "works of mercy"—direct service to the victims of injustice—there are both the variety of material or financial support projects described in chapters 5 and 7, and the possibilities of standing or working side-by-side with the people that Witness for Peace (chap. 4), pairing (chaps. 2 and 7), and work brigades (chap. 7) represent. In terms of the "works of justice" or structural change—working to change the situations, policies, or institutions that create victims in the first place—there is analysis of and public education about U.S. policy (chap. 1) and the variety of political action responses that are an essential part of the Witness for Peace effort and pairing projects in particular. On the level of personal lifestyle, the solidarity buying projects described in chapters 6 and 7 provide opportunities for simple, ongoing links with Nicaragua, as do the pairing projects

INTRODUCTION 3

and the more interior or spiritual dimensions of solidarity (chap. 8), particularly prayer and fasting. This dimension, the "inner core of solidarity," is an essential source or nurturing element in our solidarity work and gives a completeness or integration to our solidarity work that can sometimes be lost in the demands of the projects themselves. Visually, this integrated response can be presented as in Diagram 1.

Diagram 1

An Integrated Response to Nicaragua

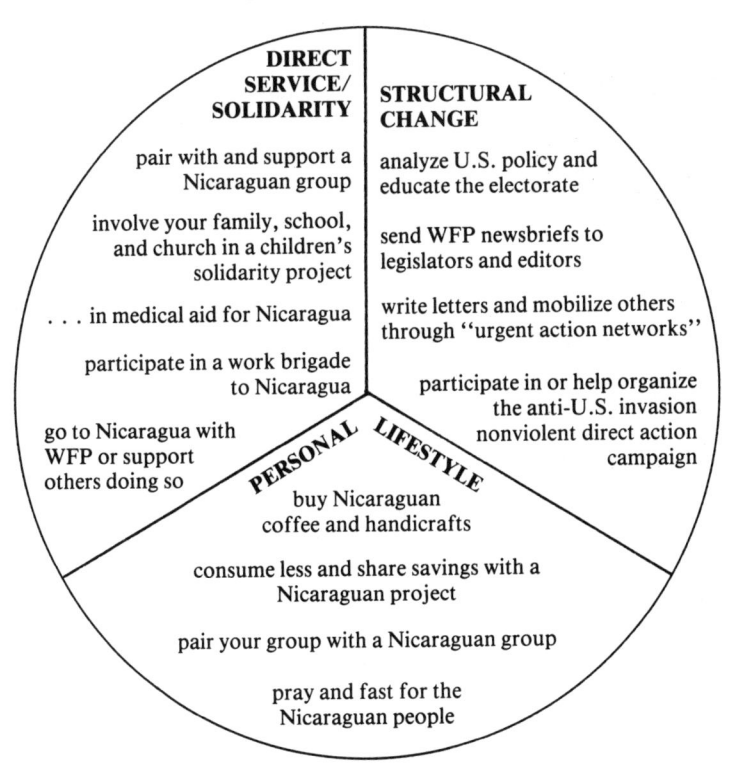

DIRECT SERVICE/SOLIDARITY
- pair with and support a Nicaraguan group
- involve your family, school, and church in a children's solidarity project
- ... in medical aid for Nicaragua
- participate in a work brigade to Nicaragua
- go to Nicaragua with WFP or support others doing so

STRUCTURAL CHANGE
- analyze U.S. policy and educate the electorate
- send WFP newsbriefs to legislators and editors
- write letters and mobilize others through "urgent action networks"
- participate in or help organize the anti-U.S. invasion nonviolent direct action campaign

PERSONAL LIFESTYLE
- buy Nicaraguan coffee and handicrafts
- consume less and share savings with a Nicaraguan project
- pair your group with a Nicaraguan group
- pray and fast for the Nicaraguan people

As part of its goal to effectively mobilize both individual and collective support for the people of Nicaragua and to challenge U.S. policy, especially the misinformation and distortions underlying that policy, this book goes beyond a description of solidarity projects and presents a glimpse at least of the Nicaraguan Revolution and process of national reconstruction. That is, each chapter and each story of Nicaraguan individuals and groups serve as an illustration of some aspect of reality or life in Nicaragua. Health care, education and the literacy campaign, the prison system, and urban barrio life in general are illustrated in the stories in chapters 2, 3, 7, and 8, especially in the story of the community of Ciudad Sandino. What the Nicaraguan Revolution looks like in rural areas, and how the current war affects the lives of the Nicaraguan rural poor, find expression in chapters 4 and 5, particularly in terms of the community of Jalapa on the Nicaraguan-Honduran border where Witness for Peace initiated its nonviolent presence in Nicaragua. Chapter 6, on the Nicaraguan coffee project, provides a glimpse of the Nicaraguan economy as a whole and the government's approach to food and agriculture in particular. The religious dimension of Nicaraguan life is seen in the groups described in chapter 3, with the story of the La Merced youth group providing the opportunity to consider the growing tension between the Catholic hierarchy and the Nicaraguan government.

Finally, the point-for-point refutation in chapter 1 of the U.S policy paper on Nicaragua speaks more analytically about many of the basic concerns raised about Nicaragua—the Miskito Amerindians, human rights issues, church-state relations, Nicaraguan foreign policy. But the bulk of the book is narrated in personal terms—stories—because its basic goal is to foster relationships, to touch hearts and deepen solidarity, so as to lead to more creative, courageous, and persevering political action.

Each solidarity project or group mentioned in this book is listed in the Resource section at the end, with addresses and phone numbers (generally omitted in earlier chapters). The lists of audiovisuals, books, pamphlets, and newsletters are not exhaustive but rather focus primarily on the issues and projects described in this book.

CHAPTER ONE

U.S. Policy toward Nicaragua

HISTORICAL OVERVIEW

Historically, the relationship between the U.S. government and the people of Nicaragua has hardly been one of solidarity. From the mid-nineteenth century to the present, the U.S. government has sought to dominate Nicaragua. Current efforts to overthrow the Nicaraguan government relate directly to its rejection of U.S. control and to the example that such an independent country offers to other Central and South American countries. Nicaraguan independence represents the beginning of the collapse of the basic premise of the Monroe Doctrine—that the Western Hemisphere "belongs" to the United States.

To understand better the present hostility of the U.S. government toward Nicaragua, it is helpful to single out some of the major efforts by the U.S. to control Nicaraguan affairs since the mid-1800s:

1850   The U.S.A. and Great Britain, without consulting Nicaragua, sign the Clayton-Bulwer Treaty, declaring that both nations will share rights to a trans-Nicaraguan canal.

1855   U.S. adverturer William Walker is invited by liberal Nicaraguan interests to head up their forces against conservative elements. He is successful and has himself declared president of Nicaragua in 1856. Partly because of confiscating property controlled by tycoon Cornelius Vanderbilt, he is forced to surrender to the U.S. military in 1857.

1909 Nicaraguan President Zelaya resigns because of U.S. anger over his canceling U.S. concessions for a trans-Nicaraguan canal.

1912 The first of nine invasions of Nicaragua by U.S. marines, who occupy the country for most of the next twenty-five years.

1927 Augusto César Sandino begins his six years of armed resistance to the U.S. marines, who are unable to defeat him.

1933 The U.S. government agrees to withdraw its marines, but only after creating the Nicaraguan National Guard headed by General Anastasio Somoza, who has Sandino executed in 1934.

1935 to 1979 The Somoza dynasty rules Nicaragua as a dictatorship with the support of the U.S. government. President Franklin Roosevelt once said: "He [Somoza] may be a son-of-a-bitch, but he's *our* son-of-a-bitch."

1961 The FSLN (*Frente Sandinista de Liberación Nacional* Sandinista National Liberation Front) begins armed resistance and political organization. Its popular base widens in the early 1970s, and many grassroots Christian communities, forming especially in rural areas, give it their support. In 1977–78 the Nicaraguan Catholic Church, the business community, and the opposition press side with the FSLN in opposition to Somoza. In July 1979 it is successful in overthrowing the dictator, despite U.S. efforts through the Organization of American States to retain "Somocismo" (a client relationship with the U.S.A.) but without Somoza.

1979 to 1980 The Carter administration provides $75 million in aid, trying to work out a constructive relationship with the revolutionary government, but all such aid is terminated when Ronald Reagan becomes president.

1982 "Covert" aid, in the amount of $19 million (President Reagan wanted more), to "contras" (anti-Sandinista guerrillas), is allocated by Congress for channeling by the

CIA. For 1983 the figure was $24 million, with a March 1984 request for an additional $21 million denied by Congress.

CURRENT U.S. POLICY

In June 1982, I interviewed the director of public affairs at the U.S. embassy in Managua. I asked him what was the official U.S. policy toward Nicaragua. He gave me a copy of a two-page "gist," as it was called, as the best short statement available through official channels:*

The U.S. and Nicaragua, April 1982

A quick reference aid on U.S. foreign relations, not a comprehensive policy statement—Bureau of Public Affairs, Department of State.

Background: Toward the end of the Nicaraguan civil war, the OAS passed a resolution in June 1979 calling for "immediate and definitive replacement of the Somoza regime"; "guarantee of the respect for human rights of all Nicaraguans without exception"; and "the holding of free elections as soon as possible, that will lead to the establishment of a truly democratic government that guarantees peace, freedom, and justice." In a letter to the OAS in July 1979, before assuming power, the Provisional Government of National Reconstruction promised to "install a regime of democracy, justice, and social progress in which there is full guarantee for the right of all Nicaraguans to political participation and universal suffrage"; "guarantee the full exercise of human rights and fundamental freedoms"; and organize "a mixed economy."

The Sandinista leaders have reneged on these promises. They have ignored a basic tenet of the inter-American system—nonintervention in the affairs of other states—by providing material and other support for subversion in El Salvador and elsewhere.

---

* It is interesting to note that when parts of the statement appeared in a Nicaraguan newspaper in late June, the U.S. embassy denied that such a statement even existed and called it a fabrication of the newspaper.

Nicaragua also is engaged in a rapid arms buildup which threatens the security of its neighbors. Rather than strengthening democracy, the Sandinistas have concentrated on consolidating political power, imposing heavy constraints on opposition activity and postponing elections. This trend led Eden Pastora, a founder and popular hero of the Sandinista movement, to break publicly with them in April 1982, accusing them of betraying their promises of freedom and progress. The economy has done poorly despite more than $125 million in U.S. aid and several hundred million from other Western donors. Production is well below prerevolutionary levels. Largely because of the regime's hostility, private internal and external investment is almost nonexistent.

Intervention in El Salvador: Nicaragua is the support and command base for the Salvadoran guerrillas. Arms and supplies are received in Nicaragua and transhipped by land, air, and sea to El Salvador. The guerrillas' Unified Revolutionary Directorate has its headquarters near Managua; with the help of Cuban and Nicaraguan officers, it coordinates logistical support, including food, medicine, clothing, money, and munitions, and selects targets to be attacked. Salvadoran guerrillas move through Nicaragua to Cuba and elsewhere for training; some training is conducted in Nicaragua. The Sandinistas also provide support for leftist extremists in Guatemala, Honduras, and Costa Rica.

Military buildup: Nicaragua, with a population of 2.7 million, has expanded its active duty forces to 20,000–25,000—at least twice the size of Somoza's National Guard; reservists and militia exceed 50,000. To accommodate this force, the Sandinistas have built 36 new Cuban-designed military garrisons, in addition to 13 garrisons inherited from the National Guard. In contrast, Costa Rica has no standing army, and Honduras, with 1 million more people than Nicaragua, has total forces of about 17,500. Some 2,000 Cuban military and internal security advisers are in Nicaragua, and several hundred Nicaraguan military are training in Cuba. Sophisticated weapons, including Soviet-made T-55 tanks, amphibious ferries, and transport aircraft, have been added to Nicaragua's arsenal. Airfields have been lengthened to handle MIG aircraft; Nicaraguan pilots are training in Eastern Europe. Recently, Nicaragua also has purchased rocket-launchers, helicopters, and patrol boats from France.

Attacks on pluralism: It is increasingly clear that the country is controlled by the Sandinistas' nine-member Directorate—all Marxists—and not by the government's official structures, the Coordinating Junta or Cabinet. The trend is toward a one-party state.

—Elections have been postponed until at least 1985.

—The respected, independent newspaper *La Prensa*, for years the voice of opposition to the Somozas, has been closed down repeatedly for carrying unwelcome news; *La Prensa* and independent radio news services are now heavily censored.

—Archbishop Obando y Bravo was banned from performing Mass on television, and the Catholic Church's radio was temporarily closed.

—Independent political parties are harassed and denied permission to hold public rallies; their headquarters have been attacked by Sandinista-orchestrated mobs, and their leaders have been refused permission to travel abroad.

—In October 1981, five leaders of COSEP, the umbrella private sector organization, were arrested and some jailed for four months, because they issued a statement criticizing official policy.

—Cuban-style block committes have been set up to monitor political activities at the community level.

—Three years after the Sandinistas took power, there are still some 4,200 political prisoners; allegations of political arrests and disappearances have increased.

—Tightly controlled Sandinista labor and peasant organizations have been established.

—The Sandinistas have engaged in a systematic destruction of the way of life of the isolated Miskito Indian tribe. At least twenty-six of their villages are now deserted—most burned to the ground. Some ten thousand Miskitos have been detained in "relocation" centers, and as many as twelve thousand have fled into Honduras.

U.S. policy: While the U.S. had shared the hopes for a pluralistic, nonaligned Nicaragua, we have been increasingly concerned with the deteriorating conditions and have repeatedly called "our concerns" to the Sandinistas' attention. Assistant Secretary of State Enders went to Managua in August 1981 to meet with Nicaraguan leaders. Against the background of increasing restrictions on domestic dissent, the discussions focused on the regional security problems caused by Nicaragua's military buildup and arms supply to Salvadoran guerrillas. In exchange for Nicaraguan action on our concerns, the U.S. offered resumption of economic aid and cultural/technical exchanges and assurances we would not aid groups seeking to overthrow the Nicaraguan Government. In March 1982, although the Sandinistas had demonstrated no willingness to address our concerns, Secretary Haig reaffirmed U.S. willingness to discuss outstanding issues, and in April our Ambassador presented specific proposals to the Nicaraguan Government. The new eight-point U.S. plan includes a proposed regional arrangement for arms limitations and international verification. We would welcome cooperation with a pluralistic Nicaragua committed to peace and friendship with its neighbors.

ANALYSIS OF THE U.S. POLICY STATEMENT

One of the principles on which this book is grounded is that responsible and effective concern requires political action as well as personal support of Third World groups. To be more effective in our challenging of U.S. policy in Nicaragua, we need first to understand that policy and point out the factual inaccuracies on which it is partially based.

Based on my firsthand experience in Nicaragua, on interviews with both supporters and opponents of the Nicaraguan Revolution, and on the reading I have done, I confidently conclude that the evaluation of Nicaraguan government policy in this statement is replete with factual inaccuracies and misinterpretations of reality. Because this misinformation is used to justify U.S. opposition to Nicaragua, it needs to be exposed for what it is. Space prevents an extensive, line-by-line response, but every point in it can be challenged, including the innuendos contained in some of the vocabulary.

1. "Nonintervention in the affairs of other states"—specifically in reference to El Salvador. As of the autumn of 1984, every attempt of the U.S. government to produce proof of Nicaraguan involvement in El Salvador has backfired. In February 1982 the U.S. embassy staff in Nicaragua was asked by a group of

Church World Service personnel from the U.S.A. about the date of the most recent evidence that the U.S.A. had of Nicaraguan arms shipments to El Salvador. The answer given was April 1981. The director of public affairs was asked why the U.S.A. has not revealed the evidence it claimed to have and why the U.S.A. has not agreed to the invitation of Nicaragua to send a joint team to monitor the supposed transfer areas. He replied: "If the arms are being shipped across on a Tuesday at a certain location and we go there on a Tuesday, they would have shipped them across somewhere else on Sunday. They're not dumb!"

In reality the United States has massively intervened in El Salvador and now Honduras is intervening as well. Apart from the U.S. blatant disregard of the "basic tenet of the inter-American system," the U.S. response to undisguised Honduran intervention in El Salvador has been to provide it with more arms and more military training, and to lengthen the runways of its airports to accommodate U.S. aircraft to be used to intervene in Central America!

2. Nicaragua's "rapid arms buildup, which threatens the security of its neighbors." The U.S.A. is not trying to hide its massive arming of the Honduran military, which in turn is supporting the several thousand ex-Somoza National Guardsmen operating out of Honduras. Every week there are border crossings, in some cases major invasions in which Nicaraguan soldiers and civilians are killed. Add to this the admitted U.S. policy of destabilizing the Nicaraguan economy, its allowing Nicaraguan exiles to conduct military exercises in Florida and California, and U.S. participation in invasions and other activities directed at "unfriendly" governments in Latin America since the 1950s, and it is obvious why there is an arms buildup in Nicaragua. But it is not one that threatens the security of its neighbors.

3. The Sandinistas are "consolidating political power . . . and postponing elections." The Sandinistas are definitely consolidating political power. They are determined to make the revolutionary process work and not allow the fifty thousand persons who died in the Revolution to have died in vain. But they are not consolidating political power by eliminating their opposition; they are consolidating political power by the effectiveness of their efforts to meet the needs of the people and cope with the multiple

crises confronting the country. The government seems to be tolerant of church opposition—for instance, by allowing opposition clergymen to say practically anything from the pulpit. The government commitment to literacy for every Nicaraguan is hardly consistent with stifling opposition, especially when viewed against Somoza's commitment to keeping the rural poor illiterate as part of his explicit strategy for minimizing his opposition.

National elections were moved up to November 4, 1984—five years after the Revolution. This allowed time for the critical tasks of national reconstruction to have the full attention of the country, time for educating an illiterate peasantry and for potential political leaders to demonstrate their real concerns for the people. The first U.S. elections were held in 1789—six years after the end of the Revolutionary War.

4. "The economy has done poorly despite . . . U.S. aid." Somoza and his allies stripped the treasury clean and left the new government with a staggering $1.6 billion debt and a devastated country (massive bombing of Nicaraguan cities in the final weeks of the insurrection). There was no harvest that year, there was a shortage of trained personnel, and some factory owners and plantation owners deliberately sabotaged their operations. Counterrevolutionary invasions and economic sabotage divert badly needed resources from economic reconstruction to national defense. The U.S. refusal to sell badly needed spare parts to operate everything from buses to the U.S.-made machines in its textile factories is reminiscent of how the U.S.A. contributed to the economic crisis that undermined Salvador Allende's government in Chile in the early 1970s. Add to this the U.S. blocking of loans to Nicaragua from international agencies, as well as the U.S. cutoff of wheat shipments to Nicaragua. One of the saddest aspects of the supposed U.S. assistance is revealed in the U.S. response to the devastating floods of May 1982 (see below).

Yes, there is an economic crisis in Nicaragua, but not primarily of its own making. But the economy is rebuilding and basic human needs for food, shelter, health care, education, and transportation are being met, at least minimally, *despite* U.S. "aid."

5. "The regime's hostility to private internal and external investment." There has been no ceiling placed on profits in Nicaragua. There is no ceiling on the number of acres of land that

plantation owners can have, so long as they produce on that land. One private owner controls half of the sugar lands in the country and makes a good profit on his exports. What he and other capitalists do not have in Nicaragua is the political power that goes along with economic wealth in a capitalist system.

In Nicaragua, the private sector produces/controls some 75 percent (according to most estimates) of the national wealth, but it does not have 75 percent of the political power in the country. The private sector had its representative in the Council of State, the transitional national legislative body, as did each of the ten political parties in Nicaragua. But that was all.

If private enterprise wants both profits and political power, Nicaragua is indeed a "hostile" environment. But if private enterprise is willing to settle for profits alone, there is an open invitation to produce and profit in Nicaragua. The goal of a "mixed economy" (a combination of private enterprise and private farms, cooperatives, and state-controlled lands and industries) is being achieved.

6. "Intervention in El Salvador." The allegation of "support for leftist extremists" is interesting. The so-called leftist extremists in El Salvador and Guatemala, particularly, are *the people*. Oppressed for generations, brutally repressed at the present time, many of them have taken up arms as a last resort, in self-defense. Certainly Nicaragua would want to support them, just as U.S. freedom-fighters would have supported their counterparts in the French Revolution shortly after the American Revolution. But because of the position and power of the U.S.A.—just waiting for a shred of hard evidence to show that arms or personnel are involved, as an excuse for an invasion of Nicaragua—this support has to be confined more to what would be called "moral support."

7. "Military buildup." The figures given in the Bureau of Public Affairs statement are inaccurate. Nicaraguan leaders I met with in 1982 were not willing to reveal the size of their regular army, though they implied that it was smaller than the figure of 20,000 to 25,000. On the other hand, the popular militia was closer to 100,000 than to 50,000. (But because of the escalating war, these figures were probably closer to 30,000 regular army and 100,000 to 150,000 popular militia by the autumn of 1984.) Why?

Nicaraguans want to be able to defend their country. Everywhere you see the slogan, *A cualquier costo, cumpliremos con la patria* ("whatever the cost, we will do our duty to the homeland"). And you see it in their faces and in their commitment to the daily volunteer tasks of national reconstruction.

"Two thousand Cuban military"? Two hundred is the figure used by most Nicaraguans, although the Center for Defense Information (see Resources) used the figure of two thousand in its estimate for 1983, adding that many returned to Cuba in 1984. Nicaraguans training in Cuba and armed with Russian weapons? Yes. They are prepared to defend their country and want the best weapons they can afford and from wherever they can get them. They would be as happy to buy them from the U.S.A. if the U.S.A. were willing to sell them.

To imply, however, that Cuban training and Russian arms mean that Nicaragua is a satellite of Russia or a carbon copy of Cuba is totally false. The Nicaraguan Revolution and its program of national reconstruction is vastly different from Russian communism and is distinct in many ways from the Cuban Revolution and model. It is uniquely Nicaraguan, as will become more evident in this book.

8. "Attacks on pluralism."

a) Elections (see #3, above).

b) *La Prensa*. This is a complicated story and censorship is a complicated issue. *La Prensa* is not the voice of the people that it was before the Revolution, as the Bureau of Public Affairs statement implies. Its commitment to the people, as represented by its editor Pedro Joaquín Chamorro (killed by Somoza in 1978), was continued after the Revolution by his brother, Xavier Chamorro. When Pedro's son and his mother felt *La Prensa* was becoming too supportive of the Revolution, they forced Xavier to resign. Eighty percent of the staff went with Xavier to start a new newspaper, *El Nuevo Diario*. The line now followed by *La Prensa* is clearly in opposition to the Revolution. It reflects U.S. values and mores, and seems bent on discrediting the government internationally.

The censorship law forbids the publishing of lies and stories that cause economic damage. A story on a shortage of beans, for example, can lead to panic buying and thereby intensify the shortage. The law is applied to stories that would embarrass the government and thus possibly jeopardize international support. Given the very real threats that the government faces and given the economic crisis it is struggling to overcome, some censorship makes sense—although it provides an easy opportunity for those who oppose the government to call it totalitarian. Does the Revolution have a right to survive? Obviously. How far can it go to protect itself? That is a difficult question to answer. Where do you draw the line on "freedom of the press," especially when the particular press at issue seems committed to undermining the Revolution?

c) The archbishop's Mass on television. What the government apparently stopped was airing *only* the archbishop's Mass. It was willing to allow Masses of the archbishop *and others* to be televised. As with the censorship issue, this seems to be a "no-win" situation for the government, especially when the archbishop is becoming more and more hostile and, in my opinion, unreasonable, at least at times, in his opposition to the government. (See chapter 3, pp. 60–63, for a summary of the conflict between the Nicaraguan government and the Catholic hierarchy.)

d) "Cuban-style block committees." These are the Sandinista Defense Committees (CDSs). They are responsible for health, housing, sports, cultural activities, vigilance, and food distribution on each block. In their "vigilance" function, they discourage crime and protect important neighborhood facilities (counterrevolutionary sabotage is a very real threat). To imply that this means "spying" and thus some kind of invasion of privacy, as the Bureau of Public Affairs statement does, is to distort their reality. The adjective "Cuban-style" is meant to stir up repressive images that are not borne out by the reality of the situation.

e) "Forty-two hundred political prisoners" (see chapter 7).

f) "Systematic destruction . . . of the Miskito Indian tribe." This is perhaps the biggest lie of all. The Sandinistas made some very real mistakes in the first year or two regarding the Miskito Amerindians. They tried to integrate them into the national life without understanding their language, culture, and historical situation of isolation from the rest of the country and their quite different colonial history. Many young Sandinistas overreacted to Miskito opposition to government policy. A few Sandinistas and Miskitos were killed in the process. However, the forced relocation of some ten thousand Miskito Amerindians from near the Honduran border was not at all what the Bureau of Public Affairs statement implies.

Counterrevolutionary raids by ex-National Guardsmen based in Honduras increased in number and intensity in late 1981, culminating in a plan to "liberate" the northeastern corner of the country, in an operation known as "Red Christmas." Thousands of Miskito Amerindians living in that area were trapped and were being used more and more by the ex-National Guardsmen and some Miskito collaborators. A difficult military decision was made to relocate the Miskitos away from the border. It had to be done quickly and involved real hardships. Crops almost ready for harvesting and livestock were destroyed to prevent the counterrevolutionaries from taking them. In some cases the journey to new and much more productive land to the south took seven days. But hundreds of Sandinista volunteers helped to carry what possessions could be transported. Women, children, and the elderly were provided transportation whenever possible.

In the relocation centers, the government provided *all* the food until the first harvest came in. The government provided housing, built schools and clinics, and supplied teachers and medical personnel—at tremendous cost, given the serious limitation of resources in the nation. But the government was trying to show the Miskito people (and the world) that it was sincere in its effort to improve the economic situation of the Miskitos and respect their cultural traditions. On the Atlantic coast where the Miskito and two other Indian peoples as well as English-speaking Creoles live, the national literacy campaign was conducted in each of the native languages.

Everyone we met who visited or worked in the relocation centers was impressed with what they saw and agreed that the government had no other choice in a very difficult situation. Although the Catholic hierarchy issued an extremely critical document in February 1982, after rejecting government invitations to personally inspect the relocation centers, the Moravian bishop on the Atlantic coast and many other religious leaders who work with the Miskito people or who personally visited the relocation centers supported the government actions.

9. "U.S. policy." This paragraph in the Bureau of Public Af-

fairs statement is a classic "Catch 22." According to the director of public affairs in the U.S. embassy, the U.S.A. is unwilling to sit down with Nicaraguan officials to negotiate a new relationship based on the eight points mentioned in the paragraph "until Nicaragua shows some willingness to change its activities in El Salvador. Nicaragua's relations with its neighbors is our primary concern in dealing with Nicaragua. Nothing else is really that critical." But the U.S.A. apparently has no hard evidence of interventionist activities by Nicaragua in El Salvador, and Nicaragua categorically denies such activities. As pointed out earlier, Nicaragua has offered to form a joint team to monitor the border, but the U.S.A. dismisses the offer.

When asked about overflights by U.S. intelligence planes over Nicaraguan territory, and about the U.S. intelligence ship in the Gulf of Fonseca between Nicaragua and El Salvador, the director of public affairs replied: "Maybe there are overflights, maybe there aren't." As to allowing Nicaraguan exiles to conduct military training in Florida and California, he stated that it depends on how one interprets the law. The law forbidding such activities on U.S. soil applies, he said, to exiles from countries "friendly to the U.S.A." He added that the law is applied when foreign exiles actually engage in a process of invasion (the example he used was setting sail from New Orleans for Nicaragua).

When asked whether restricting such counterrevolutionary activities in the U.S.A. might be a symbolic statement to Nicaragua that the U.S.A. truly desired a cooperative relationship, the director answered: "They'd just accuse us of something else. Besides, when two parties start from such different ideological positions, what expectations can you have for fruitful dialogue?" It seemed clear that, in his opinion, the U.S. government had no hope or intention of pursuing negotiations with Nicaragua to establish a less hostile relationship.

Just how antagonistic the U.S. government is toward Nicaragua was revealed in its response to the floods in May 1982. The damage was worse than that caused by the earthquake of 1972, which focused the attention of the whole world on Nicaragua. It was as costly, economically, as the civil war itself.

After the 1972 earthquake, aid poured into Nicaragua from all over the world, especially from the U.S.A. U.S. government contributions were estimated at $76.7 million; churches and other private agencies in the U.S.A. contributed millions more. What was the U.S. response to the even greater natural disaster ten years later?

According to the U.S. embassy official interviewed, the U.S. contribution was less than $300,000 and that in the form of food supplies already in Nicaragua (warehoused at the embassy) waiting to be released for a variety of programs should the Nicaraguan government ever agree to the monitoring conditions that the U.S.A. requires of its food donations. In addition, according to the embassy official, the U.S. ambassador wrote a check for $25,000.

When asked whether the U.S. government would consider some Public Law 480 food assistance over the summer and fall when food shortages would again be felt across the country, he replied that the Nicaraguan government, from other sources, already had promises of more food than it needed. Besides, he added, "they don't *ask* for aid. They *demand* it and tell you that it is your moral obligation to provide it."*

ESCALATION OF U.S. HOSTILITY

In subsequent months, U.S. hostility escalated further. The following five events are only the most flagrant.

The Contadora Peace Process

In January 1983, Mexico, Venezuela, Panama, and Colombia secured agreement with the Central American countries on

---

* The overall picture of foreign aid to Nicaragua is revealing. According to Nicaraguan government statistics, between July 1979 and March 1982 the government received a total of some $1.55 billion in foreign aid—$130 million from Mexico, $75 million (or 5%) from the Soviet Union, and the largest amount from international development banks. Though the Russian amount is only 5% of the total, it has been most helpful. Within two weeks of the destruction of the hospital in Chinandega because of floods, Russian transport planes had delivered an entire hospital—building, equipment, and staff. Similarly, when the Reagan administration in May 1981 canceled the $30 million in wheat shipments approved for Nicaragua by the Carter administration, the Russians stepped in and provided the wheat (which, most ironically, they had just bought from the U.S.A.). Overall, 49% of Nicaraguan aid comes from other Third World countries, 32% from First World countries (mostly West European), and 19% from Second World countries (Eastern Europe and the Soviet Union).

twenty-one objectives calling for the establishment of democratic systems of government; the reduction of current inventories of arms and military personnel; the proscription of foreign military bases; the reduction and eventual elimination of foreign military advisors and troops; an end to support for subversion; and adequate means of verification and contrbl. The Reagan administration claims to support this political path to peace but its actions and even its words contradict that claim.

On September 12, 1983, Under Secretary of Defense Fred Ikle gave a speech to the Baltimore Council on Foreign Affairs in which he clearly implies that the U.S. goal is to see the government of Nicaragua overthrown:

> We must prevent consolidation of a Sandinista regime in Nicaragua that would become an arsenal for insurgency, a safe haven for the export of violence. If we cannot prevent that, we have to anticipate the partition of Central America. Such a development would then force us to man a new military front-line of the East-West conflict, right here on our continent.

Invasion of Grenada

The October 1983 U.S. invasion of Grenada made the possibility of a similar invasion of Nicaragua seem much less hypothetical, despite repeated Reagan administration denials.

Kissinger Commission Report

In January 1984, the Kissinger Commission provided a bipartisan platform for a reiteration of the Reagan analysis of and policy toward Nicaragua. As analyzed in the February issue of *Envío*:

> With respect to Nicaragua, the Commission presents a two-track policy. On the one hand, economic, military, and political pressure will be maintained with the goal of forcing the Nicaraguan government to abandon some of the basic goals of the revolution: "we do not believe that it would be wise to dismantle existing incentives and pressures on the Managua regime except in conjunction with demonstrable

progress on the negotiating front" (p. 116). On the other hand, direct military intervention could become politically viable if Reagan is re-elected or if the Salvadoran situation changes notably: "as part of the backdrop to diplomacy, Nicaragua must be aware that force remains an ultimate recourse. The United States and the countries of the region retain this option" (p. 119). The Kissinger Commission justifies this threat by alluding to Nicaragua's alleged role in the East-West conflict.

The Kissinger Commission report obviously embodies the true Reagan administration "solution" for Central America, a solution that the Contadora process has been able to fend off until now. . . . In response to this mediating role, the Kissinger Commission's position on Contadora is quite clear: "the United States cannot use the Contadora process as a substitute for its own policies," because "the interests and attitudes of these four countries are not identical, nor do they always comport with our own" (p. 120). Such a position does not rule out continued rhetorical support for Contadora and the use of that process to pressure Nicaragua, via the proposals of U.S. regional allies, while the Reagan administration continues in practice to ignore Contadora's pleas not to fan the flames of war in Central America.

The Kissinger Commission was also eloquent in expressing the Reagan administration's attitude towards its Western European allies: "we should seek their political and diplomatic support where this is possible, and their restraint where it is not. We should strongly discourage their aiding the Sandinista regime, until it fundamentally changes course" (p. 124). Serious respect for the views of those allies is not necessary, as they have only "modest economic concerns" and "occasional residual involvements" in the region, along with an "inadequate" grasp of the great questions of world security at stake (pp. 123-24).

Military Escalation in Honduras

U.S. military maneuvers in Honduras have escalated dramatically since 1982. The summer of 1983 saw several months of joint maneuvers with Honduras involving U.S. warships off both Central American coasts, and sixteen thousand U.S. military personnel, including five thousand ground troops. "Big Pine II" ended in February 1984 and "Grenadero I" began in April, involving five thousand U.S. troops. Simultaneously, the U.S.A. launched "Guardians of the Gulf," a surveillance "exercise" in the Gulf of Fonseca between El Salvador and Nicaragua and "Ocean Venture '84," a massive maritime exercise in the Caribbean Sea involving thirty thousand U.S. military personnel in a practice invasion of the Puerto Rican island of Vieques, similar to a 1981

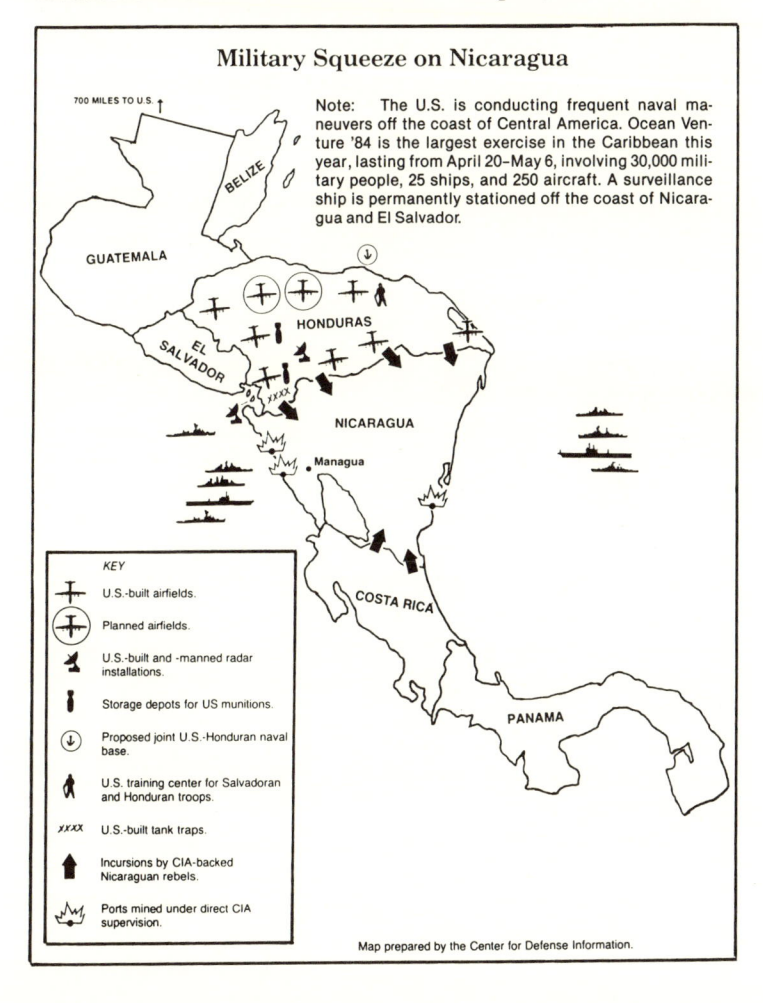

Military Squeeze on Nicaragua

Note: The U.S. is conducting frequent naval maneuvers off the coast of Central America. Ocean Venture '84 is the largest exercise in the Caribbean this year, lasting from April 20–May 6, involving 30,000 military people, 25 ships, and 250 aircraft. A surveillance ship is permanently stationed off the coast of Nicaragua and El Salvador.

KEY
- U.S.-built airfields.
- Planned airfields.
- U.S.-built and -manned radar installations.
- Storage depots for US munitions.
- Proposed joint U.S.-Honduran naval base.
- U.S. training center for Salvadoran and Honduran troops.
- xxxx U.S.-built tank traps.
- Incursions by CIA-backed Nicaraguan rebels.
- Ports mined under direct CIA supervision.

Map prepared by the Center for Defense Information.

mock invasion that proved to be the practice run for the invasion of Grenada. With each new maneuver has come additional military facilities in Honduras, additional weapons, and additional U.S. troops on what seems a permanent basis. This militarization of Honduras is well documented in both the May 1984 *Envío* and *Defense Monitor* (1984, vol. 13, #3) from the Center for Defense Information (see Resources).

Mining of Nicaraguan Ports

More and more overt U.S. support of the "contras" was coupled in February and March 1984 with the CIA overseeing the placing of some six hundred mines in Nicaraguan ports. The U.S. Congressional outcry threatened continued funding of CIA involvement (the House of Representatives rejected further aid to the "contras" in May). The Nicaraguan complaint to the International Court of Justice at The Hague was upheld; the Reagan administration refused to recognize the jurisdiction of the court.

AN ALTERNATIVE POLICY

Many nongovernment groups have analyzed U.S. policy toward Nicaragua. The Center for Defense Information, for instance, in its spring 1984 study, arrived at and published the following:

Conclusions

- The US military appears to be preparing to fight in Central America, particularly Nicaragua, despite the fact that there is no threat at present to US interests which would justify American combat intervention.
- The United States is threatening Nicaragua and promoting military solutions to the region's problems in preference to diplomatic initiatives and negotiated political settlements.
- Increased US military aid and activities will not lead to an end to the conflicts in the region, but will raise the level of violence, make political settlements more unlikely, and risk turning national conflicts into regional wars which could

ultimately involve the United States and the Soviet Union.
- American actions are perpetuating military-dominated repressive regimes, delaying necessary political negotiations, and intensifying anti-American attitudes throughout Latin America.
- The United States needs to emphasize positive, cooperative, non-military actions beneficial to all nations of the region. Serious consideration should be given to the formation of a voluntary economic federation of all North and Central American nations [*Defense Monitor*, vol. 13, #3, 1984, p. 16; see also Phillip Berryman's analysis in *Sojourners*, August 1984].

As part of what is called the "Central American Peace Campaign" (see chapter 7, pp. 142-43 for details), a wide variety of U.S. justice and peace groups, Central American groups, and Latin American experts have formulated an alternative U.S. policy for Nicaragua and Central America as a whole. This coalition, known as Policy Alternatives for the Caribbean and Central America (PACCA), has published its policy alternatives in a booklet entitled *Changing Course: Blueprint for Peace in Central America and the Caribbean*, a summary of which accents the following elements:

The Blueprint in Brief

Principles for a New Policy

U.S. foreign policy should be based on the principles which it seeks to further in the world. These include: non-intervention, respect for self-determination, collective self-defense, peaceful settlement of disputes, respect for human rights, support for democratic development and concern for democratic values. Adherence to these principles is critical to working out practical programs for regional peace and development.

A Program for Peace

To avert a wider war in Central America, the United States should take the following short-range steps:

- **Nicaragua:** cease backing the counter-revolutionary forces based in Honduras and Costa Rica, and support Contadora efforts to normalize relations between Nicaragua and its neighbors.
- **El Salvador:** cut off military aid, and support efforts for a negotiated settlement involving power-sharing among the contending forces.
- **Honduras:** dismantle the U.S. bases in Honduras, withdraw U.S. troops and warships, and participate in development aid.
- **Guatemala:** express disapproval of the government's repressive policies toward indigenous people, maintain the cut-off of military assistance, and provide aid for Guatemalan refugees in Mexico who have fled from the violence there.
- **Costa Rica:** oppose militarization and extend economic assistance.
- **Cuba:** begin a process designed to achieve normal diplomatic and commercial relations.

A Program for Development

Development based on the needs of the majority in Central America and the Caribbean should be promoted by new U.S. initiatives in the areas of aid, trade, and debt.

- **Aid:** U.S. economic assistance should flow towards those regional programs and governments that are narrowing the gulf between rich and poor, as well as to grassroots institutions and projects that diversify the economic base of each country.
- **Trade:** U.S. trade should be liberalized alongside support of limited commodity agreements to help Central American countries stabilize earnings from their commodity exports.
- **Debt:** The U.S. should support regional plans for renegotiation of external debt.
- **Workers and Migrants:** The U.S. should develop programs to compensate and retrain U.S. workers affected by liberalized imports and guarantee rights to immigrant workers.

In terms of Nicaragua specifically, the alternative policy calls for the following practical steps:

1. Cease support for the paramilitary exile groups attacking Nicaragua from Honduras and Costa Rica, and discourage other nations from providing such support.
2. Cut back the military force the United States has assembled around Nicaragua, including an end to military exercises in Honduras and off the Nicaraguan coast, and the withdrawal of U.S. combat forces currently deployed in Honduras.
3. End the effort to strangle Nicaragua's economy by blocking international credits.
4. Fully support and encourage a negotiated reduction of tension and the normalization of relations between Nicaragua and Costa Rica and Honduras. Such negotiations can take place either bilaterally or under the auspices of the Contadora Group, but should follow the basic outlines of the security proposals made thus far under Contadora's auspices, and should include provisions for adequate verification of compliance. They should also include provisions for a humane resettlement plan for those who were recruited to fight the covert war.
5. Accept Nicaragua's offer to negotiate bilateral security concerns [*Changing Course*, p. 65].

This policy alternative has been endorsed by scholars, development specialists, public officials, and leaders of church, labor, minority, and civic organizations in the U.S.A. It can become part of our political action response to U.S. intervention in Nicaragua, as we lobby for specific pieces of legislation with the help and information of groups such as the Coalition for a New Foreign and Military Policy and its legislative hot-line for Central America (202-483-3391) and engage in more dramatic forms of public education/witness and direct action (see chap. 4).

CHAPTER TWO

Ciudad Sandino and St. Louis: A Solidarity Pairing Project

THE REVOLUTION IN A BARRIO CONTEXT

The barrio of Ciudad Sandino ("Sandino City"), on the outskirts of Managua, began its story in 1969. The flooding of Lake Managua drove hundreds of families to a large cotton farm owned by a man who decided there was more profit in selling plots of land to flood victims than in growing cotton. Many considered this resettlement area the worst slum in Managua because of the total lack of services. For the first few months after the flood, everyone lived in tents; afterward they began to build small shacks.

After the 1972 earthquake in Managua, thousands more homeless Managuans fled to this area, then called OPEN 3 (*Operación Permanente de Emergencia Nacional*; there were two other resettlement areas, on the eastern fringe of Managua). After this large new influx, residents began organizing to campaign for basic services—water, electricity, bus service, and a cemetery.

The 1976 campaign for water was a significant turning point in the history of this community. At stake was a 300 percent increase in the price of water, which the residents refused to pay. The struggle was publicized in *La Prensa*, then a growing voice of opposition to General Somoza's regime. OPEN 3 was becoming a national symbol of resistance and popular organization.

The cemetery struggle solidified this resistance even more. When the government refused to provide land for a communal cemetery, the residents took over some land and buried two of their dead infants. When the National Guard came in and dug up the bodies, everyone was furious. Many more residents joined the armed opposition to Somoza and OPEN 3 was, the scene of several major confrontations with the National Guard in the last two years before the victory of the Revolution on July 19, 1979.

After the victory, OPEN 3 was renamed Ciudad Sandino, with a population of about 45,000, with another 15,000 to 20,000 persons living in surrounding villages. Administratively, it is divided into nine zones and is governed by a barrio committee composed of representatives of each of the zones. This committee of nine decided to have an election to choose one of its members to serve as a full-time paid coordinator, so that an official barrio office could be open during the day to conduct transactions with the various Managua ministries providing services to the barrio. Five leaders from each of the nine zones were chosen to vote in the special election conducted one Sunday afternoon in one of the five schools of the barrio. The nine zones in Ciudad Sandino are subdivided into 224 block organizations—Sandinista Defense Committees (CDSs).

For the most part, adults have only a 4th-grade education. But there are now four large primary schools, two of which are also secondary schools, with an enrollment of over two thousand each, divided into three daily shifts in each school—morning, afternoon, and evening. One of them is a Catholic school, but in addition there are three smaller Protestant primary schools and many small preschools.

A large new market now serves the population. There are three bus routes but only the main street is paved. Water and electricity are available in all the zones, and banking services are also available. Although Ciudad Sandino is a residential area, there are now many factories located on the highway leading to the barrio. Many barrio residents are employed in them. In addition, there are a lot of small "home industries" in the barrio. For those who have permanent jobs, the monthly salary level varies from U.S. $28.50 to $90.

Ciudad Sandino workers are artisans, carpenters, drivers (bus and truck), market vendors, teachers, nurses, domestic workers, mechanics, seamstresses, beauticians, small store owners, laundry women, bread bakers, tortilla makers, broom makers, brown-bag makers, shoe-shine boys, shoe makers and menders, police, militia, army personnel, food vendors, small mill owners, watchmen, bank employees, newspaper vendors, tailors, cotton and coffee pickers, furniture makers, electricians, plumbers, cement-block, tile, and washtub makers, condiment and candy makers, television and radio repairers.

Religion

As to religion, Ciudad Sandino is composed of at least three major groups. There are zones in which Jesuit priests are very supportive of the revolutionary process and encourage participation in it by their parishioners. There are also zones in which other Jesuits are supporting the growing opposition of the Catholic hierarchy to the revolutionary process. And there are many Protestant "street-corner" churches where the predominant stance is one of otherwordliness and noninvolvement with the revolutionary process.

The Juventud Sandinista (Sandinista youth movement) is very active in Ciudad Sandino, participating in every national campaign. It was especially helpful during the terrible May 1982 floods. The ECR (Revolutionary Christian Students), less militant than the Juventud Sandinista, was also active in the barrio Catholic school until the Franciscan Sisters were removed by the hierarchy.

Health Care Services

Probably the best way to see how Ciudad Sandino functions and what the revolutionary process means in practice is to examine its health care system.

The State and the People

Ciudad Sandino has a "unified health system" in which the Ministry of Health and popular organizations work together to bring health care to the people, to implement the August 1979 law declaring that "health is a right of all the people and the responsibility of the state and the organized people." The participation of the Ministry of Health in this unified system is best illustrated in the clinics of Ciudad Sandino. The participation of popular organizations or the organized people is best illustrated by the work of the *responsables de salud* ("health administrators," i.e. volunteers responsible for health issues at the zone and block levels, hereafter abbreviated RS).

Before the Revolution, there was one clinic in OPEN 3, open five mornings a week, staffed by one doctor and one nurse. Since the Revolution, two more clinics have been added and the total number of personnel for the three clinics (including secretaries) has jumped to sixty-five. But some of these staff members are still imbued with the kind of professionalism learned in prerevolutionary medical and nursing schools. They will not, for instance, make house calls when necessary—in the opinion of the Maryknoll sisters living and working in Ciudad Sandino. The sisters describe the Ministry of Health in Managua as the worst of all the ministries, in terms of the number of "Somoza leftovers" in middle-management positions.

The FSLN retained large numbers of personnel from the Somoza era primarily because of the severe shortage of trained persons, and because of the FSLN commitment to a policy of national unity. But this has entailed some motivational disadvantages, and things are moving more slowly than they should.

However, despite these and other problems (no telephone in the main clinic until 1984, only one ambulance for the entire barrio—and it can spend weeks in a repair shop—and no facilities at all for nighttime emergencies), the clinics are providing significantly more health care than before the Revolution. A 30-bed maternal-child hospital is in the planning stages.

The main clinic is housed in the home of a former Somoza official, expanded to accommodate a dental clinic, a well-baby room, a vaccination room, a small lab for simple tests, a room for medical records, and a small room for the health environmentalist. Adjacent to the building was a small piece of property that the community converted into a well-baby facility—with local labor and materials, and the help of outsiders.

In 1982, the clinics charged one córdoba (about 4 cents) for consultation with a doctor, to provide such items as soap that can otherwise take as long as three months to get by requisition from the Ministry of Health. That money has also paid for a roof over the walkway where persons line up at noon for the results of their lab tests (one to two hours of noon-day sun in the tropics is a lot). But now all consultations are free. Dental clinic services are also free, except for shots of Novocain, which cost ten córdobas (compared with 100 to 150 córdobas in private dental offices). Clients start lining up for numbers for morning appointments at 6 A.M. and others come at 9 A.M. to get numbers for afternoon appointments.

In a country experiencing a scarcity of resources, little is wasted. In the clinic lab, match boxes serve as containers for fecal specimens, and urine specimens are to be found in baby food jars. The environmental health office handles such things as cleaning up stagnant water (where mosquitoes breed) and the distribution of latrines (25 latrines are supposed to come from the Ministry of Health each month, but the schedule is several months behind). The office is also responsible for handling complaints about animal health hazards (e.g., pigs and cows roaming the streets and spreading infectious diseases). A 1984 law requiring that all pigs be kept in backyard pigpens has resulted in a marked decrease in the number of pigs roaming the streets.

The People

The other half of the health care system in Ciudad Sandino is the responsibility of popular organizations—the people. At the head of this system is the People's Health Council, composed of the clinic director, a health educator, a representative of the nurses, representatives from all the popular organizations (AMNLAE, the women's association; Juventud Sandinista; and others), and two "health administrators" (RSs). The People's Health Council meets every two weeks to deal with the official programs of the Ministry of Health, with issues raised by the popular organizations, and with its own health care projects.

The two RSs on the council represent the People's Health Commission. This commission is composed of the nine RSs who are responsible for the nine zones into which Ciudad Sandino is divided administratively. It is these nine zonal RSs who are the key to the entire system and who provide a real glimpse into how the revolutionary process is working.

These nine RSs are all volunteers, generally full-time, which means evenings as well as days, whenever there is a health emergency in their particular zone. Eight are women. The ninth is a man who works out of his own home and is thus available to his neighbors during the day. Of the eight women, one is a single woman of 42, another is a student, and the other six are mothers in their 30s (one is also a grandmother). These are persons who have a history of community involvement in Ciudad Sandino and several are members of the basic Christian community (*comunidad de base*) in their parish.

The responsibilities of these nine RSs are enormous. Each is part of the leadership group of their particular zone (besides health care, there are leaders for housing, civil defense, defense of the economy, and publicity) and thus participates in a range of zonal decisions. They are responsible for the participation of their zone in national health campaigns (making sure that all workers have the supplies they need, know their areas of responsibility, and are motivated). The RSs are also responsible for environmental health issues in their zones, such as making sure that streets are as level as possible, to prevent stagnant water from pooling. They handle the distribution of food supplements to malnourished infants and expectant and nursing mothers in their zone. This involves three hours of their time each afternoon and extensive record-keeping, to ensure that the recipients are using the food supplements properly and are reporting to the clinic for regular check-ups.

Zonal RSs are supposed to work one day a week at their clinic and some have taken responsibility for ensuring that the proper supplies of basic foods are available in their zones. This latter operation is coordinated nationally by a government agency called ENABAS. ENABAS is a coordinated series of national, regional, and local distribution centers for basic foodstuffs such as beans, rice, flour, sugar, and oil. These items are distributed in rural areas and urban barrios through local stores that agree to provide these items at a price set by the government. If the participating stores in a given zone do not have their allotments, it is the zonal RS who gets on the phone to the ENABAS outlet in Managua.

The final responsibility of the zonal RSs is the animation and coordination of the RSs from each of the block CDSs in their zone. There are about 25 block RSs for each zonal RS. In addition, each block is supposed to have at least one *brigadista de salud* ("health promoter") to assist in the national health campaigns. Most of the *brigadistas de salud* and many of the block RSs are high-school students. The block RSs are responsible for house-to-house visits, referrals, and the like, in their block. However, because most of them are full-time students, they do not have the time for such visits and this task often falls back on the zonal RSs. In the first five years of the Revolution, there were so many mobilizations for so many things—vaccinations for polio and DPT, two or three different antimalaria campaigns, periodic neighborhood clean-up efforts, the national literacy campaign, flood relief, training and participation in the popular militias for each neighborhood, and neighborhood vigilance—that many persons were simply wearing out. The zonal RSs and the popular organizations, particularly AMNLAE, have the responsibility for counteracting this phenomenon among their block RSs and *brigadistas de salud*.

A good example of the strengths and weaknesses in this system was the national antidengue campaign of July 11, 1982. Every clean water container in the country was to have a tiny packet of disinfectant dropped in it, to kill a particular type of mosquito. For Ciudad Sandino, this meant wrapping 54,000 portions of the powdered disinfectant in pieces of cloth, and distributing the packets to the block RSs and *brigadistas de salud* who had previously conducted house-to-house surveys to determine the number of fresh water containers in each house, and who would distribute these packets on July 11. Preparing 54,000 packets is not an easy task. Normally it would be the block RSs and *brigadistas de salud* who would volunteer for the task. But because they had missed two weeks of school working on flood relief in late May, their semester exams had been moved back to the first two weeks of July. These exams are crucial and neither students nor their parents were willing to jeopardize them. Thus, the zonal

RSs began a frantic search for other volunteers, and on the Tuesday before July 11, some 30 elementary school students and 35 adults (including several of the zonal RSs themselves, along with clinic personnel) spent all day wrapping packets of disinfectant. The zonal RSs reflected on this experience and were quite self-critical about their failure to involve all five elementary schools in the process. They themselves were feeling overwhelmed by all that had needed to be done in the past several months.

Maura Otero

The driving force behind much of this effort in Ciudad Sandino is a woman name Maura Otero, *responsable de salud* (RS) for zone 4. The story of the revolution is precisely the story of persons such as Maura—their own transformation and what they give to their neighborhood and country.

Her day begins at 5 A.M., so that she can be at the main clinic from 6 to 7 A.M., to pass out numbers for the morning appointments, and from 8 to 10 A.M. for the afternoon appointments and any problem-solving that arises. She is expected to do this only once a week, but ends up doing it almost every day because the other four zonal RSs assigned to the main clinic are unable to take their turns. Between 7 and 8 A.M. Maura is back home preparing breakfast for her husband and others living with them. Her husband is a taxi driver who supports her revolutionary activities. He is involved in the taxi cooperative in Managua but not in any of the mass organizations. From 2 to 5 P.M. she is home for the distribution of food supplements for her zone. One of the walls of her living room is lined with 25-pound sacks and assorted other containers. During other times of the day she visits some of the 900 homes in her zone, especially the 270 households that receive food supplements at her door. Her four children are all grown up, the youngest being a 19-year-old son serving in the army. She has one of her grandchildren and two other relatives living with her in a temporary foster-care arrangement. Record-keeping for the food supplements takes up another part of her day.

When I asked how she does it all and what motivates her, she replied: "During the insurrection all my children were involved. I didn't do what I knew I should, because I was afraid. Now I have to make up for that." The pictures on her wall of Jesus and Fr. Gaspar García (a Sandinista priest-leader killed during the insurrection) reveal other sources of her strength and faith.

Maura Otero (left) and a co-worker
wrapping packets of disinfectant

The story of the revolution is precisely the story of persons such as Maura—their own transformation and what they give to their neighborhood and country.

"Some persons did not believe at first that Maura was doing all this as a volunteer," explained Maryknoll sister Bea Zaragoza. "They were sure that she must be getting paid. But over the months they have come to see that she is for real."

Says Maura: "Many of my neighbors used to complain about

the food shortages, how they couldn't get what they needed. But now that's beginning to change, as we explain why the shortages exist. More and more they are getting involved. It moves slowly, but it's moving."

A Mental Health Team

Sometimes things move very quickly and spontaneously in Ciudad Sandino (and in Nicaragua in general). One such example was the formation of the mental health team. A Maryknoll sister volunteered to come to Ciudad Sandino two days a week to share her psychological skills. At the same time, an Argentine psychiatrist showed up to volunteer two days a week in Ciudad Sandino. He was on a 3-year service contract to work at the psychiatric hospital in Managua, and he wanted to do more. Julianne Warnshuis, a Maryknoll sister with training in special education, joined the others, as did also a social worker and a psychiatric nurse—all in the course of the spring of 1982. They offered their services through the local CDS structure and were assigned to the main clinic. As a result of their work, a "day hospital" was opened in 1984, built by the patients themselves as part of their occupational therapy.

Julianne's special education work became an "early education" program for physically and mentally handicapped children from birth to age 6. She presented the need for a better program for these children to the Ministry of Education. She was named its first coordinator and has now been replaced by a Nicaraguan university student. With the help of several university students and local women, a survey was taken to discover the various disabilities and children needing help in the barrio. Once the number of children was determined, "promoters" were to be assigned a certain number of families to work within their homes.

The "promoter's" work is to instruct parents on how to work with their own children, with the goal of incorporating the child into a regular school by the age of 6. If this is not possible, then the child would be enrolled in the Special Education School in Managua. But with only two minimally paid promoters for a community of more than 60,000, the team found itself often doing whatever little emergency work it could, in hopes that eventually the economic crisis in Nicaragua would improve and provide at least some limited funding to address serious problems at a causal level. In 1982, Julianne worked with a number of children with language deficiencies largely due to being left alone all day because their mothers have to leave for work at 4 A.M. It was real neglect, but there did not seem to be a realistic alternative for most mothers.

Day-care centers are one alternative, but again the problem is that of a grave shortage of resources. Day-care centers have been declared a national priority. But the limited national budget means that Ciudad Sandino was allotted only one center for 45,000 residents, half of whom are under 15 years of age. This center opened in March 1984 and handles 120 children. Trained personnel is another aspect of the national problem. The two special education schools in Managua are staffed by teachers who have had no more than a one- or two-month training course in Panama or Costa Rica.

"People here do what they can with the little training the country can afford to give them and they pass that little on to others," Julianne explained. "I hope that some day soon we will have the luxury of sending persons away for the proper training. Meanwhile, we do the best we can with what we have. It's amazing how much is getting done with so few resources."

Literacy Campaign

One of the major ongoing accomplishments of the Revolution that is especially evident in Ciudad Sandino is the literacy campaign, in particular the follow-up adult education program. After the initial 5-month campaign in 1980, Popular Education Collectives (CEPs) were set up, each under the guidance of either the teacher of the locality or a newly literate student, who became the CEP "coordinator" to continue the education of other newly literate adults. These coordinators receive continued instruction from promoters of the Ministry of Adult Education. This continuing adult education ranges from the introductory level to the 6th level (a somewhat specialized primary education).

By 1983 the Program of Adult Education in Ciudad Sandino had its own office. A Catholic sister from Venezuela, Isabel Sánchez, oversees the program, with three assistant technicians, for five zones in the barrio. In 1983, the beginning enrollment was 642 students; 400 finished the school year. In 1984, almost 700 adults were enrolled in the program, which involves two hours of study each Monday through Friday. The "oldest" students are now entering the 5th level.

Because of such efforts at the local level in many Nicaraguan communities, especially because of the participation of hundreds of thousands of volunteers in a country with a population of less than 3 million, the health care and education situation has changed dramatically in only a few years. Statistically, as Table 1 reveals, the situation three years after the Revolution was very different from one year before the Revolution.

Table 1

Education and Health Care in Nicaragua

	1978	1982
Illiteracy rate	50.35	12.07
Education expenditure thousands of córdobas	341,024	1,159,876
Percentage of GNP for education	1.32	4.25 (1981)
Total students	501,660	1,000,103
Adult education students	none	242,587
Infant mortality	191/1,000 births	94/1,000 births (1981)
Vaccinations	810,000	1,740,000
Health budget (córdobas)	373,000	1,231,000 (1981)

Source: *Envío* 13, Instituto Histórico Centroamericano, Managua, July 1982, *Programa Bienestar Social* (health expenditures), reprinted from *What Difference Could a Revolution Make?*, with permission of the Institute for Food and Development Policy.

Maryknoll in Ciudad Sandino

The inspiration radiated by persons such as Maura Otero and the hundreds of other Nicaraguans in Ciudad Sandino has deepened the commitment of the Maryknoll sisters living and working with them. In fact, Maryknollers have been with this community from the beginning. Maura Clarke, the Maryknoll sister martyred in El Salvador, spent a number of years in Ciudad Sandino and is honored there by a park named after her and a monument on the street where she lived. Bea Zaragoza has been in Nicaragua since 1958 and in Ciudad Sandino since its beginning. She has been working with the *comunidad de base* in her parish and is now assisting Maura Otero with all the tasks she has in zone 4, especially the home visits and follow-ups that are not getting done because most of the block RSs are students in school.

Joining the Maryknoll sisters in July 1982 was a Maryknoll lay mission team—Don and Celine Woznica. Don is a doctor and works in the clinics. Celine assists as a paramedical professional and also works with Salvadoran refugees in Managua.

Part of the work of this Maryknoll team is with a basic Christian community in their zone. It is composed of a core group of about twenty to twenty-five members, all but five of whom are women. They gather on Saturday evenings for Scriptural reflection and prayer. A planning group prepares the sessions, which follow a program that integrates the Scriptural reflection with the reality of the reconstruction process the Nicaraguan people is living through. In its desire to be of service to the wider community, the group has been visiting elderly persons in a Managua nursing home.

Bea's comment when asked why the group did not involve itself in the neighborhood tasks of the CDSs as their way of doing "Christian service" was very interesting: "Oh, they are already doing that—participating in the mass organizations. They don't consider that special. They are also looking for ways of serving others less fortunate than themselves—the works of charity or mercy."

It is especially with these persons—the Maryknoll team, the *comunidad de base*, Maura, and the other health *responsables*—that North American groups should associate themselves if they decide to make the efforts of Ciudad Sandino a part of their own work for justice. Bea Zaragoza has promised to be the liaison between Ciudad Sandino and any North American groups desiring such a direct linkage. Write her at Apartado P-165, Managua, Nicaragua.

Maryknoll lay volunteer Don Wozuica
in the lab at Ciudad Sandino's main clinic

Part of the work of this Maryknoll team is with a basic Christian community in their zone. They are looking for ways of serving others less fortunate than themselves—the works of charity or mercy.

THE PAIRING

A link between Ciudad Sandino, Nicaragua, and St. Louis, Missouri, began to be forged in the fall of 1982. Members of a

Parenting for Peace and Justice family support group in St. Louis (eight families working together to make peace and justice more a part of their own family lives and doing some outreach locally to other families) viewed some slides of various Nicaraguan groups listed at the end of this book (see Resources). Later that fall, the group decided to contact Maryknoll Sister Bea Zaragoza, the liaison person for the group in Ciudad Sandino. Bea responded favorably and the St. Louis group planned a special "Nicaraguan Family Night" for January 9, 1983.

Each St. Louis family brought stationery, envelopes, pictures, and other family momentos to a pot-luck dinner, prepared in part by a local native Nicaraguan, Adela Peuguet. The dinner consisted of various rice and bean dishes, plus Adela's special Nicaraguan casserole. Before dinner, the adults and children saw slides on Nicaragua and Ciudad Sandino in particular. Maps and Nicaraguan posters around the room also helped visually.

After dinner each family had two tasks. Some family members composed a letter of concern to the White House about U.S. policy toward Nicaragua, with copies to their representative and senators, and a copy for the group in Ciudad Sandino. Other family members affixed pictures and family momentos onto two pieces of construction paper to make a short story of their own family. These eight stories (16 pieces of paper) were then combined into a group album and sent to families in Ciudad Sandino.

The letter-writing and album-making was followed by some Nicaraguan dances. With Adela's help, the group learned some simple steps and had a lot of fun in the process. It was a fun experience as well as a serious solidarity project. Reflecting back on this family night, one of the families involved put it this way:

> For our two daughters, who were 4 and 7 at the time, the Nicaragua Night was an especially good experience—it was fun! It was a good exercise in trying to communicate creatively who we are as a family and as individuals. We chose various pictures to send and our daughters helped choose them. We also wrote our letter in Spanish. This pairing experience has reinforced our desire to have the girls learn Spanish. It seems to us that being able to speak another language is one piece in building transcultural bridges. And

because of this pairing relationship, the girls perceive the word "Nicaragua" as a place that has some meaning, not simply as a funny sounding word.

It was several months before any of the St. Louis families heard from Ciudad Sandino. What Bea Zaragoza had done was to take each of the eight family stories in the group album and give it to a particular Nicaraguan family in the base Christian community where she was working. Initially, three of the Nicaraguan families responded with letters. Bea had paired my own (McGinnis) family with Maura Otero's family, and it was Maura's letter that arrived first and let the group know that the pairing was really happening. A letter from Maura was special because of her role in the community and especially because of the relationship established with her during my initial visit to Ciudad Sandino in 1982.

Maura's letter also provided more information about her health work and about the needs of the main clinic. She asked if we could collect a number of medical and educational supplies (everything from marking pens, staplers, and staples, to bandages and baby scales). This was discussed at the next monthly meeting of the family support group. The adults decided to involve the children as much as possible by asking each family to decide what supplies it would be willing to find and then to bring them to a special picnic. The adults felt it would be a richer experience for the children if they could see all the supplies collected and realize that in working together more can be done and more joy experienced. The picnic was scheduled for the same day as a special "Peace Pentecost" service, so that the families could go from the fun event to a more serious prayer vigil together.

The supplies filled four very large boxes, thanks to donations from a medical supply company. The next question was how best to get the supplies to Nicaragua. Negotiations with airlines and transport companies stretched out over several frustrating months. Finally, more than six months later, the supplies began to be taken to Nicaragua by Maryknoll sisters traveling from New York to Managua.

During 1983, besides the medical supplies effort, the pairing relationship expressed itself primarily through correspondence. Although not every St. Louis family heard from a Nicaraguan family (letters were lost in the mail), and although letters were not very frequent from either side, bonds of solidarity were beginning to form. As for my own family, having a picture of Maura and her family on our "shalom box" (a shoe box decorated with pictures of times and ways we have built or experienced shalom as a family) on our dinner table beside a small Nicaraguan flag (from our local UNICEF store) has reminded us to pray for peace for our friends in Nicaragua as part of our dinner prayer. Further, each family had been given a map of Nicaragua and several pictures of the people and community of Ciudad Sandino at the "Nicaraguan Family Night." Posting these as a collage on the wall in our breakfast room has also served as a reminder of our special relationship with Maura and Ciudad Sandino.

For another family, it has been a picture of their Nicaraguan family on their refrigerator that serves, in their words, "as a reminder of the family of God all over our world":

> We tune in our ears and eyes to the television and newspaper when anything about Central America is mentioned, because now we feel we know someone there in a special way. In the months ahead, we hope to continue to be ever more informed about the issues in Central America. We are reading Henri Nouwen's excellent article (*America*, April 21, 1984) on "Christ in the Americas" and want to spend more time sharing all of this with our four children.

As U.S. involvement in Central America, especially in Nicaragua, escalated over 1983, each St. Louis family was increasingly concerned, and this concern translated itself into action. First, as the "sanctuary" movement for Salvadoran and Guatemalan refugees in the U.S.A. grew, the group decided to consider how it could relate to this effort. After several months of reflection, each family committed itself to some specific support activity. One person raised the whole issue with his United Church of Christ congregation where he was associate pastor. Others collected clothing and other items for Salvadoran refugees coming to St. Louis. Several agreed to provide short-term "refuge" for any Salvadorans on their way elsewhere. All decided to spend an evening (meal plus visiting) with the first Salvadorans provided sanctuary in St. Louis.

Secondly, group members became more involved politically, particularly in political letter-writing and in inviting others to share in this urgent task. As one family put it, "Before, Nicaragua was just another country in turmoil somewhere south of Mexico. Its people were distant. But because of this pairing relationship, that distance disappeared and we found ourselves much more active."

Another family elaborated on this point:

> To our surprise and delight, a package was delivered to us shortly after Christmas 1983, along with a letter from a family and some totally unexpected gifts for our children. Sue and I felt overwhelmed by the generosity of these people. We were almost surprised to learn that our paired family was attempting to lead a normal life: attending school, raising a good-sized family, and working, while actively supporting their country's fight for autonomy and change. We were touched by their commitment and disheartened by our own leaders' seeming lack of understanding in dealing with Nicaragua. We found that so few of our friends were aware of or could define the situation objectively. As a result of these experiences, our family has become more involved in telling others about Nicaragua and trying to learn more about Central America as well. During peace Sunday in February, we were asked to speak to our congregation of the United Methodist Church about our involvement. We shared our gifts and experiences and told of the effort to raise money for the "Playgrounds, Not Battlegrounds" project [see chap. 5]. Our children have taken an active role in finding aluminum cans for a recycling project, the money from which we have used to purchase items to send to our family in Ciudad Sandino. Jennifer and Jeff have taken their gifts to school and have been asked many questions by both students and teachers. We hope to continue our communications with the Velázquez Cerrato family in order to deepen our understanding of their situation. Perhaps in

some small way we can also help others understand that the people are the real victims of the civil wars in Central America. We feel that we in the United States must try to extend hope to our brothers and sisters there and help our political leaders see the human side of this war.

The third response of the St. Louis group to increased U.S. intervention in Nicaragua was expressed through the Witness for Peace (WFP) program (see chap. 4). Several members of the group were supporting other persons in the St. Louis area who were planning to go to Nicaragua as part of WFP, but no one of us had considered going ourselves. But with the invasion of Grenada, a similar invasion of Nicaragua seemed an imminent possibility, and the desire and need for urgent responses became clearer.

I decided I had to consider the possibility seriously. Dramatic action to mobilize public opinion in the U.S.A. clearly seemed called for, as well as in-person expressions of solidarity for the Nicaraguan people. "The Nicaraguan people" was no longer an abstract mass for us, but specific individuals with whom we as a group were relating. But what is an appropriate response for those with family responsibilities? As a spouse and parent, what risks are justified? On the other hand, Nicaraguan spouses and parents take risks all the time. True, but should not individuals without immediate family responsibilities be the first to go?

These reflections were brought to the December 1983 meeting of the family support group. Beautiful things happened that evening. In discussing risk-taking, one person exclaimed, "Isn't this why we came together in the first place—to enable one another to take risks that we wouldn't be able to take on our own?" Later, another person said that her family would be "family" for ours while I was gone, and each family represented there that evening agreed to be "family" on one of the days I would be away. Finally, the group decided to combine a December 22 Christmas carol evening with a "commissioning service" should our family decide to send me to Nicaragua after Christmas as part of WFP.

It was a difficult decision but eventually the whole family agreed that I should go. The local WFP group decided that a money gift should accompany the group going to Nicaragua. After consulting with Nicaraguans connected with WFP, a $4,000 goal was set to purchase toys for the 4,000 children of Jalapa (see chap. 4). This project was shared with the family support group and the commissioning service on December 22. Several families put together Christmas packages to be hand-delivered to their partner families in Ciudad Sandino. A dentist in the group collected some dental supplies for the community dental clinic.

The orientation in Managua for the WFP team was arranged to include an afternoon in Ciudad Sandino, so that the various expressions of solidarity could be made in person. Visiting with Maura and her family and several of the other families was a special experience. And it was a real delight to find the pictures of our children on Maura's living room wall. This visit also enabled the Nicaraguan families to have their letters and gifts collected and hand-carried back to the U.S.A.

This exchanging of gifts has been a very important dimension of the pairing relationship. As one of the St. Louis families described it:

> Our Christmas 1983 mailing list now included our new family in Nicaragua. Because of the WFP trip, our annual family letter and some small presents could be delivered to Nicaragua. When we received presents from them, we were deeply touched. These were meaningful objects for our home and a tape of their life and views of the present struggle to be free. Supportive words were said of the present leadership in Nicaragua. There is a similar ring in what we say to each other—that peace, justice, and freedom are precious commodities. These are yearnings of our hearts and souls. The pairing has surely brought this to light for us.

Another dimension of the pairing relationship that is beginning to develop, partly because more persons are traveling between St. Louis and Nicaragua who can hand-carry items, is an exchange of reading materials. The Nicaraguan families have taken the lead, sending periodicals describing important aspects of the new society they are building, as well as newspaper clippings on current happenings. As a result, some of us have had opportunities to improve our Spanish. And some of us are becoming more careful to clip and send articles, political cartoons, and other write-ups on local solidarity efforts as well as on national concern for U.S. policy toward Nicaragua.

Although each group's difficulty in speaking and reading the other's language limits the extent of the information-sharing, it is the solidarity-sharing underneath the information-sharing that is just as important. This was beautifully expressed in a letter from the Velázquez family in Ciudad Sandino:

> It is useful for us to have your friendship by correspondence even though we don't speak the same language. We have

Part of the Velázquez family

"With these words, 'A free country or death,' we say thank you, compañeros, for your solidarity, and we will keep on praying and struggling for peace in the world."

received this friendship and felt it to be a revolutionary "shot-in-the-arm" because we feel more animated to go forward with our revolutionary process. The solidarity which you give us strengthens us to go ever forward because we know that the "yankee-enemy of humanity" is not the North American people but the government, because the people identify with the struggles of the *pueblos*. With these words, "A free country or death," we say thank you, *compañeros*, for your solidarity, and we will keep on praying and struggling for peace in the world.

FURTHER DIMENSIONS OF PAIRING

As will become more and more evident in the discussion of other pairing projects in the course of this book, pairing is much more than just another international "pen pals" project. Each of the Nicaraguan groups or communities in question is involved in the struggle for justice. Partnership in that struggle for justice is what pairing is all about.

One reason for pairing with Nicaraguans is to support them in their efforts. North Americans can do this best not only when we can tell them that we are praying for them but also when we can share with them the concrete ways in which we as individuals and as groups in North America are ourselves working for change, for justice. This support or inspiration needs to be mutual. We support them by our efforts to remain faithful to our own call to work for justice and peace, and we, in turn, are supported and inspired by their efforts for justice and peace—efforts that often entail risk and danger.

The purpose of such a relationship is primarily mutual support and inspiration—not ultimately a way of raising money for social change or community development projects in the Third World. However, such possibilities might arise in the course of an ongoing relationship. If so, care needs to be taken to ensure that paternalistic attitudes do not begin to erode the fundamental mutuality on which a truly beneficial pairing relationship must be based.

Although letters of support, exchanges of pictures and news articles, and possibly even some visiting of one another are helpful, perhaps the most effective help that we North Americans can provide to our Nicaraguan partners is to address the policies of our government that affect their lives. Political action is a vital dimension of a pairing relationship.

On other issues, we sometimes do not write to our policymakers or visit our legislators simply because motivation is lacking. Love would provide what is missing. The more we experience a bond with disadvantaged persons, the more we will be willing to work with them in pursuit of justice. Thus, I believe that by pairing with a specific group of Third World persons and sharing *our* struggles and other parts of our lives with them, and receiving similarly from them, we will deepen the bonds that inspire us to take action.

One course of action for North American groups to take would be that of becoming a channel for the story of their Nicaraguan partners. The lack or suppression of information or deliberate misinformation about countries such as Nicaragua is a serious issue. In agreeing to pair with a particular Nicaraguan group, North Americans should seek to publicize the efforts of that group as widely as possible. This could mean letters to the editor of one's local newspaper, inserts in church bulletins or student newspapers, reports at parish council, student government, or parent-teacher meetings, and so on.

Lastly, in terms of overall goals, there is the danger for North Americans of focusing our attention on the Third World in such a way that we overlook situations of injustice in our own neighborhoods and nation. There are "Third World peoples" (e.g., Hispanics, Vietnamese refugees) and "Third World pockets" (e.g., Appalachia) in our very midst. To bypass such people and realities because overseas relationships seem more interesting or exciting would be a distortion of what this project is all about. Thus, North American groups are asked to consider the possibility of a three-way relationship—linking up with a North American group experiencing injustice and working for change, as well as with one of the groups described in this book.

There are some practical suggestions to keep in mind when pairing, to make the experience as beneficial as possible. First, North American groups are urged to subscribe to one or more of the newsletters listed in the Resources section of this book and be in touch with national or local Nicaraguan support groups, as a way of getting information on Nicaragua. Secondly, it would be important to evaluate the pairing relationship each year, to make sure it is serving the needs of both groups. Make any changes that seem helpful. Thirdly, although some Nicaraguan groups have English-speaking persons helping with correspondence, most if not all of the correspondence should be in Spanish. If this necessitates getting translators from a school Spanish class, for instance, this should be seen as an opportunity to involve others in the project. Finally, be patient with the mails. It may take several weeks for letters and packages to arrive. Consider having letters and packages hand-carried, through such groups as the Witness for Peace teams going to Nicaragua. Also, Nicaraguan youth groups, as described in the next chapter, would appreciate having their North American partners cover the cost of their mailings from Nicaragua; they generally have no way to cover such costs.

CHAPTER THREE

Nicaraguan Christian Youth Groups: Youth Pairing Project Possibilities

BARRIO MONSEÑOR LEZCANO YOUTH GROUP

The basic Christian youth community in the parish of the Sacred Heart in Managua calls itself the *comunidad juvenil cristiana de base Francisco Javier Zeledón*—named after one of its members killed by the National Guard during the final weeks of the insurrection in 1979. Willmer (the leader), Armando, Edwin, Donaldo, Fernando, Clarisa, and Estrella all live in Barrio Monseñor Lezcano in northwestern Managua. To understand their work, it is important to understand their barrio.

Barrio Monseñor Lezcano is one of the largest in Managua, counting 10 percent of the total city population of 400,000. There are some middle-class blocks, but for the most part the barrio is relatively poor. A third of the streets are still dirt and become rivers during floods.

In Barrio Monseñor Lezcano is found a mixture of everything —from the hundreds of little stores, the many clinics, an occasional gas station, a Sandinista union office, to a multinational operation such as the Mennen factory and a corner pinball-machine hangout.

A closer look at Barrio Monseñor Lezcano reveals some of its history during the insurrection. The block where I lived—a mixture of tiny wooden shacks and an occasional large (6-room) brick home—was named after two boys who were killed on June 14, 1979 (by one of the many bombs dropped on the barrio by Somoza's National Guard). The family was in the street when the plane was spotted. The parents told their boys to run into the house and hide under the bed, but the bomb fell directly on their home.

Next door, 11-year old Nadir lives with his mother. Each day between three and six P.M. he can be found in the street playing soccer with his friends. Nadir attends a public elementary school two blocks away. Resources are sorely limited, but the spirit among students and staff seems high. Each morning the whole school assembles for the national anthem, a pledge of allegiance, and a word of encouragement from their principal. Developing a sense of commitment is crucial, for in a few years these children will be performing important roles in their society. Nadir is a member of ANS, the Sandinista Children's Association, where he learns the kinds of things one would learn in a Boy Scout program in the U.S.A. Nicaragua is a country of young leaders, with the members of the parish youth group already in critical leadership roles in their barrio.

Barrio Monseñor Lezcano is divided into three major zones, with each zone divided into some seventy-five blocks. Each block has its CDS, Sandinista Defense Committee; it meets weekly. This committee is made up of residents of the block who take responsibility for health, vigilance, food distribution, housing, culture and sports, block cleanliness, and the like. Each CDS elects its coordinator and periodically the coordinators meet. Occasionally the whole zone comes together to acknowledge the contributions of its leaders and to recommit itself to the difficult tasks of national and neighborhood reconstruction.

Clarisa

Clarisa, a member of the parish youth group, was *responsable de salud* ("health administrator") in 1982 in her own CDS, as well as health coordinator for eight other blocks in her zone. Her responsibilities included all the national health campaigns and making sure the stores in her neighborhood received their allotted supply of basic foodstuffs. She also saw to it that garbage was picked up. These tasks engaged her full-time attention, which meant that she had to drop out of college for the year.

Clarisa, at 22, is now a first-year student in social sciences at UNAN (the National Autonomous University of Nicaragua) and is one of the student directors of UNE, a student organization. She is a member of the teacher organization ANDEN, and teaches special education classes to mentally retarded 6- and 7-year-olds. She continues to be a leader in the parish youth group, is secretary for the Dominican Justice and Peace group in Managua, and continues to be active in her barrio CDS but with less responsibility.

Clarisa's whole family (mother and three brothers) has been heavily involved in the process of reconstruction. Her brother Byardo was in the mountains for eight months with the popular militia. He returned home safely and now works at a farm production center. Like tens of thousands of other Nicaraguan youths, he had to drop what he was doing and contribute more immediately to the defense of his country. More than 100,000 Nicaraguans serve in the popular militia, which enables the country to keep its regular army relatively small (30,000 according to most estimates). I met Byardo in 1982 when he was one of the leaders in Barrio Monseñor Lezcano. It was at a neighborhood assembly, where he had the responsibility for acknowledging the contributions of the various block leaders in his zone.

Many of the young persons and the older leaders as well are beginning to experience burn-out—their tasks are overwhelming. But the determination to complete the Revolution is still there. In view of how many have given their lives, they could not slacken their efforts. Clarisa was not the only member of her parish youth group at the recommitment assembly. All the group leaders were there because they are all involved in the neighborhood organizations through which they carry on their social action.

This zonal assembly took place in the parish hall of the Sacred Heart church; its Dominican priests from Spain have been supportive of the Revolution and process of reconstruction since 1977. At a Sunday Mass, the words to the children making their first communion included a reference to Christian service. Members of the youth group led the liturgical music. The theology reflected in the Sunday sermons can be characterized as a "theology of life." "Christ came that we might have life and have it abundantly" reads a notice on the church bulletin board.

One of the priests responsible for this orientation is Padre Manolo, the priest who helped start the parish youth group in 1978. Shortly after the victory in July 1979, the archbishop of Managua tried to expel Manolo from the country because of his open support of the Revolution. He was called a communist and only the massive outcry of support from the barrio, as well as from all over Managua, kept him in Nicaragua, but he was transferred to the northern city of Chinandega where he now teaches in a high school.

The members of the youth group readily acknowledged Manolo's importance in the formation of their group and their own personal spiritual formation. As is the case with most Christian youth groups in Nicaragua, the Francisco Javier Zeledón group comes together for faith reflection and for planning its involvement in parish activities. Besides participating in parish liturgies, some of them teach catechetics; others are involved in Bible study courses, a workshop on handicrafts for parishioners, and hospital visits.

Their social action, however, is mainly expressed through the revolutionary organizations in their barrio. They do not want to set up a parallel Christian organization. Rather, they and others choose to integrate their Christian perspective into the popular organizations. These young persons, 17 to 23 years old, speak of their "revolutionary Christianity" and of themselves as "Christian revolutionaries."

Their social action involvement has been extensive. In addition to Clarisa, every one of them participated in the national literacy campaign, spending five months in the rural areas of Nicaragua teaching illiterate *campesinos*, rural poor, how to read and write. Between March and August of 1980, more than 100,000 of these Nicaraguan youths put aside their studies in order to share their skills and to bring the cities and the countryside of Nicaragua together as never before. As a result, the illiteracy rate in Nicaragua dropped from an estimated 58 to 12 percent.

Estrella

Twenty-three-year-old Estrella is in her third year of economics after being trained as a secretary. In the literacy campaign, she was assigned to the department of Jinotega in northern Nicaragua, where she worked with ninety-five *campesinos*. Once a year, she returns there, to visit her best students who took over as "alphabetizers" or teachers during the follow-up phase of the campaign. Her brother had also been a *brigadista* at age 13. Her oldest sister María was killed fighting the National Guard when she was 22.

Estrella's family is the story and hope of the Nicaraguan Revolution. Doña Romelia, Estrella's mother, works with AMNLAE, the national women's organization named after a young revolutionary woman killed years earlier. Right before the triumph in 1979, Doña Romelia was working with mothers whose children were involved in the fighting or who had been killed. It was difficult for many parents; they could not understand their children's willingness to risk death. They had adapted to Somoza, to some extent, but their children had refused to adapt to his repression and injustice. Doña Romelia visited her daughter three times during the literacy campaign. "Every Sunday," she said, "buses would be packed with mothers going to visit their *brigadistas* in the field." Besides her AMNLAE work, Doña Romelia is the "health administrator" for her block.

Her husband is manager of maintenance at a local United Fruit Company plant. He has worked there eighteen years and is part of the popular militia from his neighborhood. For the last fourteen years, the plant has had a union, which he characterized as "a bourgeois company union that has stayed in power because of bribes." He is part of a Sandinista core group that feels it will eventually win the right to represent the workers of his plant. The present union, he says, makes it difficult to participate in the revolutionary process. Workers who have been summoned to a month of training as members of the popular militia have been told their jobs would not be there when they returned. Lawyers have helped to get some of them reinstated. When the members of the popular militia from his plant requested a truck to allow them to participate in the reenactment of the tactical retreat to Masaya (June 26), they were given the oldest truck and no gas. "But because some us were plant supervisors," he said, smiling, "we were able to get the gas."

Estrella and her parents,
with a picture of her sister María on the wall.

*Estrella's family is the story and hope
of the Nicaraguan Revolution.*

Doña Romelia and her husband are proud that their parish is so involved in the life of the "secular" community. Unlike some parishes in Managua and elsewhere in Nicaragua, Sacred Heart and its youth group are fully integrated into the life of the community around them. Nadir's mother Velia, for instance, is employed in a 6-person clothing cooperative located on the parish grounds. This integration of faith and action, Christianity and revolutionary activity, is not always an easy task, but it is a challenge to which these young persons and some of their parents have committed themselves. They are anxious to share their efforts to live out this challenge and commitment with North American groups.

LA MERCED YOUTH GROUP

The *comunidad juvenil cristiana de base* in La Merced parish in central Managua began in 1976, but, according to one of its leaders, it did not begin very well. By 1978 there was a core group that published a small bulletin and was involved in some religious and service activities. After the uprising in the Amerindian community of Monimbó in the nearby city of Masaya in 1978, members of the group became more involved in the opposition to Somoza. They were involved in helping to repair the damage done in their neighborhood by the National Guard. Their bulletin became more and more an opportunity to publicly challenge the government, although they knew that the National Guard was getting copies of the bulletin. Some of the members took up arms against Somoza during the last year of the insurrection.

After July 1979, these young persons turned, as they put it, to the reconstruction of their country: "to put behind us the destructive aspects of the insurrection and give Christian testimony to a new Nicaragua." This Christian testimony expressed itself in a variety of ways. Every member of the group joined the national literacy campaign. All of them are involved in some way in one or more of the mass organizations through which the reconstruction of Nicaragua is being accomplished. Ivette and Maibell, each 20 years old, are both part of a woman's brigade in the army reserves, for example. They see clearly the necessity of being prepared to defend their country and identify with the example of Fr. Camilo Torres, the Colombian priest-sociologist who took up arms in the 1960s with other revolutionaries in his country. The pictures of Fr. Torres and martyred Archbishop Oscar Romero of El Salvador hanging on the walls of their meeting room say a lot about how they understand their Christian faith.

The group is also actively involved in a number of parish activities. Their overall goal, as they expressed it, is "the integral formation of youth—involvement in the revolutionary process and reflection on this involvement in the light of the faith." More concretely, this means that they want to build a church that is alongside the poor. As steps in this direction, they have helped to organize Bible study classes in which adults and youth work together. Some of them have organized classes in sewing, others teach guitar or have conducted theater weeks for parishioners. Members of the group include Eduardo, one of the original organizers and clearly one of the leaders. At twenty-five, he is one of the "old-timers" in this group where ages·range from sixteen to twenty-five. Ivette looks her twenty years, but speaks with a maturity far in advance of her age. Articulate, determined, respectful, but clearly not at all deferential, she described her involvement in the literacy campaign and led the discussion of how any "linkage relationship" with North American groups should be conducted.

Argentina is one of the adults who works closely with the youth group. She stressed that it had been the example of the youth of the parish that led the adults to consider their involvement in the reconstruction of the country. A second adult there was Felipa. She recounted how several of them were involved in carrying messages around the barrio during the insurrection and in sheltering armed resisters. She described their arrangement of secret meetings in churches between reporters and young freedom-fighters as an experience reminiscent of the "church of the catacombs." Her comment on the 1982 flood disaster also said much: "Although the floods were destructive physically, they were constructive humanly. They brought us together even more."

In subsequent discussions, the maturity of their Christian faith amazed me. One comment particularly stood out. Pointing to the picture of Christ at one end of their meeting room, one young man declared: "Our Christ isn't the one on the wall or the one on the church crucifix. We see him in each person we meet on the street. We see Mary in each of the women of this country. . . ."

The priest working with this group is Father Antonio Castro. As a native Nicaraguan, he is under strong pressure to be "loyal" to the archbishop and cease his activities in support of the revolutionary process.

Fr. Antonio's pastoral work is divided between the parish and the Centro (Ecuménico) Antonio Valdivieso (CAV). The parish of La Merced is located in a typical Managua barrio. Within its boundaries is one of the many Managua resettlement areas created after the 1982 floods destroyed homes closer to nearby Lake Managua. Fr. Antonio was able to get some funding from outside sources to purchase the materials for some of this reconstruction, but the labor had to be donated by the community. At the Masses one Sunday in June 1982, lay parish leaders appealed to each family in the parish to have at least one family member donate the following weekend to help in reconstruction. A spirit of service is obviously widespread in his parish.

Fr. Antonio's other assignment, at the CAV, involves him in education, leadership training, Biblical reflection groups, and writing. Named after a sixteenth-century Nicaraguan Catholic

Eduardo, Maibell, and Father Antonio Castro

They are "one with the people in Christ for the construction of a new society."

bishop who was martyred because of his work with local Amerindians, CAV offers workshops on group progress skills for the young leaders of Nicaragua. Fr. Antonio's own work centers more on the promotion of the *comunidades de base* for both adults and youth and on the whole process of faith reflection by them on their involvement in the process of national reconstruction. Occasionally he writes for one of the several publications of CAV. *Amanecer* is the CAV monthly Spanish-language magazine offering analyses of aspects of the revolutionary process in Nicaragua as well as faith reflections on this process from a radical Christian perspective.

CAV is very supportive of the revolutionary process. Some have accused it and two other Christian organizations involved in "popular education" of being uncritically supportive. The challenge of working alongside the people and leadership of a country in the face of tremendous pressure as well as monumental tasks and at the same time maintaining a critical distance—refusing to identify any given historical process as the embodiment of the kingdom of God—is difficult. But it is clear that the members of the *comunidad juvenil cristiana de base* in the parish of La Merced have accepted this challenge. As they put it, they are *unidos con el pueblo en Cristo por la construcción de la nueva sociedad* ("one with the people in Christ for the construction of a new society").

In terms of a linkage relationship with one or more North American youth groups, these young persons were quite clear in terms of what they hope would come from such a relationship: that both groups share not merely information about the activities for justice and peace they are involved in, but especially faith reflection—how each sees these activities in the light of their Christian faith; that North American groups send information about Nicaragua from their own sources and information about solidarity efforts they are involved in; and that North Americans share the information they receive from Nicaragua as widely as possible. North American groups interested in a pairing relationship—a central theme of this book, to be developed at greater length in subsequent chapters—should write to Fr. Antonio Castro, Centro Ecuménico Antonio Valdivieso, Managua, Nicaragua.

THE NICARAGUAN GOVERNMENT AND THE CATHOLIC HIERARCHY

The conflict between the Nicaraguan government and the Catholic hierarchy is an involved issue, one that concerned me greatly. In its regard I interviewed many persons—religious leaders supportive of the Revolution, religious leaders opposed to the Revolution, and government officials. My major impressions can be spelled out in five parts:

1. The conflict is not between the government and Christianity, but between the government and most of the members of the Catholic hierarchy. I interviewed Archbishop Obando y Bravo at length about the conflict and what could be done to lessen tensions and promote greater cooperation. His reply to this concern was: "A committee of three bishops was initially appointed to dialogue with the government, but this proved ineffective. They are guerrillas and are guerrillas in their language and, besides, guerrillas aren't interested in dialogue. Their words are strong. They are Marxist-Leninist, of this there is not doubt, and they will remain that way."

Several other religious leaders pointed out that the person appointed by the government as liaison coordinator with religious groups is Carlos Nuñez, one of the most educated (and upper-class) members of the FSLN leadership. It was in December 1981, they further pointed out, that the government and the Catholic hierarchy agreed to a process of collaboration and dialogue, a promise to consult each other in private before going public with a disagreement. However, it was only two months later that the Catholic bishops broke the agreement and published their highly critical document on the Miskito Amerindians. For this and other reasons I do not hesitate to use the term "unreasonable" to characterize the response of the Catholic hierarchy to the government. Others use much harsher words.

2. A new sense, vision, and role for the church is being created in Nicaragua, as elsewhere in Latin America. The expression "accompanying," rather than "leading," the people—supporting the people as it expresses its faith through participation in popular organizations—points to a new model of church. For many "old

style" leaders, this is a difficult model to accept. But many Christian lay and religious leaders in Nicaragua are implementing this model and urge their bishops to support such expressions of it as the *comunidades de base.*

3. Compounding the problem is the fact that one of the traditional functions of the church in many societies, including that of Nicaragua, has been extensive involvement in helping persons to meet their basic needs—health care, education, social relationships, and occasionally housing and food. But today in Nicaragua, the government and the popular organizations have taken responsibility for these areas. However, Catholic schools still exist and are even subsidized by the government to keep tuition at a point where the poor as well as the wealthy have access to private education.

4. Lay and religious leaders working for a new sense of church are also generally very supportive of the Revolution. In fact, as illustrated by each of the youth groups described in this chapter, participating in the revolutionary process has become an important, and in some cases the primary, way of living out their Christian faith. Many Christians see the kingdom of God being built in Nicaragua and openly speak in such terms. But some church representatives feel that the critical Christian stance toward any historical process is being eroded by an overidentification with the revolutionary process in Nicaragua. The archbishop went further in his characterization of the Antonio Valdivieso Center (CAV) and two other Christian education and research institutes: "they are trying to 'Marxize' the people." My experience with all three organizations gave me a very different impression.

5. Some Nicaraguan and North American religious leaders in Nicaragua are also convinced that the Catholic hierarchy by and large reflects its own economic base and proclivity. As they said, "When the business community opposed Somoza, the bishops opposed Somoza. When the business community initially worked with the Revolution in 1979 and 1980, so did the bishops. When the business community began to oppose the revolutionary process, the bishops began to oppose it as well."

Since the summer of 1982, tension between the government and the Catholic hierarchy has escalated, with only occasional breakthroughs toward some kind of constructive dialogue. First, it was a matter of accusations of government repression of religious freedom and education, because of a personally compromising incident involving the archdiocesan director of communications and subsequent disturbances between government opponents and supporters. Then priests supportive of the Revolution were transferred from their parishes. One parish resisted the transfer and a bishop was slightly injured in the process of removing the Eucharist from the parish church. The visit of Pope John Paul II to Nicaragua in April 1983 added fuel to the fire, when his message and actions turned out to be more political than pastoral, and reinforced the growing opposition of the hierarchy to the government.

A draft law not recognizing conscientious objection gave Archbishop Obando y Bravo an opportunity to use a moral and human rights issue to express his political opposition to the government, claiming that the Sandinistas were not a legitimate government and the army not a national army but an army only of a particular political party and ideology. Then there was Bishop Schlaefer's confusing exodus to Honduras in December 1983 with a thousand Miskito Amerindians, which the Archbishop compared to Moses leading his people from slavery to freedom.

The growing opposition between the government and the Catholic hierarchy was expressed most forcefully and destructively (in terms of possible future dialogue) in the bishops' Easter 1984 pastoral letter. Ironically the theme of their pastoral was reconciliation, but the reconciliation called for was that of the government with the counterrevolutionaries. Five months earlier, the government had declared an amnesty for all Miskito Amerindians involved in the counterrevolution, but despite Bishop Schlaefer's involvement in that amnesty, the Easter document remained silent about this and other government efforts at reconciliation. And nowhere in the document did the hierarchy condemn U.S. intervention or speak of the bishops' own need for reconciliation. Instead, they urged the government to reconcile itself with the former National Guardsmen and other "contras" and allow them to participate in the November 1984 elections. Given what the "contras" are all about, the government clearly (and reasonably, in my estimation) rejected such an admonition.

This increasingly harsh opposition to the government is not only further dividing government and hierarchy but hierarchy and members of the Nicaraguan Catholic Church. Not that all Catholics oppose the bishops. Some support them. Many are confused. Some, especially young Catholics, are writing off the church. Members of the basic Christian communities throughout the country are saddened and angered by the hierarchical opposition, have challenged it, and continue to work with the revolutionary process as being clearly, in their opinion, an expression of their Christian faith. Where all this is leading is not clear, but one thing is clear: the churches in Nicaragua are struggling to discover what it means to be "church."

AN ECUMENICAL CHRISTIAN YOUTH MOVEMENT

The MJCI *(Movimiento Juvenil Cristiano Interdenominacional)* was organized on March 2, 1980, under the auspices of CEPAD, the Evangelical Committee for Aid and Development. In 1983 it was reorganized in independence from CEPAD. According to its constitution, MJCI has three basic objectives:

1. To promote Christian unity and ecumenical fellowship among youths, in order to better proclaim the kingdom of God and God's justice to all persons, especially to young Nicaraguans.

2. To offer an opportunity to Christian youths in Nicaragua to come together for reflection and enjoyment.

3. To orient Christian youths in Nicaragua to their responsibilities in the new Nicaragua *(la nueva Nicaragua)*.

Organizationally, the MJCI has a national coordinator, a national executive council, and a general assembly of all members around the country. There are also regional and local coordinators who guide the work of specific youth groups organized at the local level. More than ten Protestant churches are involved, including the Church of the Nazarene, the Church of God, the Moravian Church, the Assembly of God, the Baptist Convention, and several Pentecostal groups.

In contrast with many of the other members of these churches, these young persons are very much involved with the revolutionary process in Nicaragua. Not all of them are members of popular organizations, but all of them participate in some way in the reconstruction of their country. I came to know some of their national leaders, and it is their individual stories that I want to share. Their lives provide a number of insights into Nicaraguan reality and it is these young persons whom North American groups would be supporting by entering into a pairing relationship with the MJCI.

REVOLUTIONARY-CHRISTIAN YOUTH LEADERS

Emanuel Martínez G.

Emanuel is a founding member of the MJCI and a member of the national MJCI executive committee. He belongs to the Esmirna Baptist International Church. For six years he has been a member of the official body of this church, serving as deacon, secretary, treasurer, superintendent of the Sunday school, and president of its youth society. He has also taught in the Sunday school. Currently, he divides his time among theological studies, an evaluation project for CEPAD (studying its pastoral programs around the country), his MJCI responsibilities, and working with popular organizations. An intense young man of twenty-five, Emanuel describes himself as "a student and worker. All of us students are workers in Nicaragua." Of his work with the Revolution, he writes:

> I maintain good relations on an individual level with the mass organizations in my barrio in the work of the revolution. I fought in the armed struggle before the triumph and have been on the side of the FSLN for five years—working alongside the people, both Christian and non-Christian.

Just how intense his involvement had been during the insurrection became clear as we looked through a beautifully illustrated narration of the whole Revolution. His commentaries on the pictures and description of the National Guard came forth with such feeling. "Beasts! They were beasts!" With equal intensity he spoke of his desire to be a "brother" to North Americans. And when Emanuel said *hermano* (brother), it had a sacred ring to it.

Walter Samuel Diaz N.

Samuel took up his residency as a doctor at the Lenin-Fonseca Hospital in Managua, specializing in medicine for men, after two years of social-service medicine in the countryside (in Nueva Guinea). During the 1980 national literacy campaign, he and other medical students served as *brigadistas de salud* (health promoters) in rural Nicaragua. His last three years of medical study were spent in Managua, but the first three years had been in León, the scene of intense fighting during the last two years of the Revolution. During those months, Samuel recalled, his professors increased the amount of work, apparently trying to discourage student involvement in the insurrection. Says Samuel of his own feelings at the time, "At first I was reluctant to get involved, but then I began to work in one of the clandestine health stations for wounded freedom-fighters in León." With the MJCI, he serves as a member of the national executive committee and was enthusiastic about the idea of linking with North American Christian youth groups.

Sergio Rivas P.

Sergio is a member of La Hermosa, an Evangelical church associated with the Assembly of God. With his church, he is responsible for the Sunday school and serves as the secretary general of the church. More specifically, his work is with youths—organizing and training them toward "discipleship." He defined this role as "transmitting to youths on a personal level the various tasks they can perform within the revolutionary process." He spends time with them analyzing the situation within their church as well. In the MJCI, Sergio is currently national president and works closely with the national executive council in "the concientization of our Christian youth." Like the others, he is involved in the popular organizations. Specifically, in the university where he is studying agronomy he works with the Student Union of Nicaragua (UNEN) and in the Sandinista youth movement known as *19 de Julio* (July 19). This work, he says, "involves me in concientizing youth to its role in Nicaragua."

Javier Torres B.

Javier works in a television and radio repair shop and belongs to the National Evangelical Four-Square (Pentecostal) Church, in which he serves as advisor/counselor for the National Council of Youth. He described his overall goal in terms quite similar to the others—"how to live our faith and help young persons live their faith within the revolutionary process." In the MJCI, of which he was a founding member, Javier was the coordinator of the national executive council. In his barrio, he was secretary of his Sandinista Defense Committee (CDS), a member of *19 de Julio*, and of the popular militia. His understanding of Christian discipleship is expressed in a poem presented in chapter 8, p. 148, below.

Orlando Pérez V.

Orlando is 24 years old. Unlike the other youth leaders I interviewed, he had been confined to a wheelchair for twelve years. A swimming accident at the age of 12 left him a paraplegic. He lived with his mother and sister halfway between Managua and Masaya—a move necessitated in 1978. Because of his opposition to Somoza—from a wheelchair—the family was advised to move from Managua.

For the past eight years Orlando has been writing poetry. With encouragement from the Ministry of Culture, headed by Fr. Ernesto Cardenal (one of Nicaragua's two greatest poets), Orlando has been trying to get his poems published (see chap. 8, pp. 146–47, below, for one of his poems). Many of them were written during his six months of study in Cuba. He read selections of his poetry with great feeling. His warm face invited friendship and his prayerful presence was soothing. Several times during various meetings, he would probe me on the faith basis of my work. At the conclusion of my visit to his home, he invited the oldest person present to pray on behalf of us all.

Part of Orlando's work with the MJCI focuses on his special situation. He has been selected to represent Nicaragua at a special Latin American church youth conference where his specific responsibility is to develop a pastoral statement on the situation of persons with physical disabilities. He is an active member of the

Organización de Revolucionarios Deshabilitados (ORD, Organization of Disabled Revolutionaries; see the Appendix at the end of this chapter).

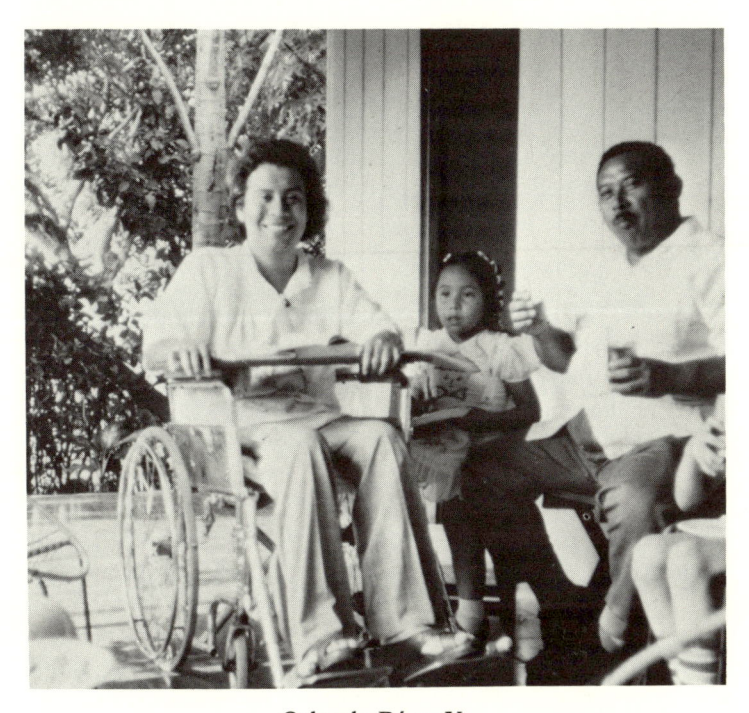

Orlando Pérez V.

Because of Orlando's opposition to Somoza—from a wheelchair—the family was advised to move from Managua.

THE MJCI AND CHRISTIAN UNITY

Each month, the national office of the MJCI puts out a Scriptural reflection for its member groups, combining a biblical passage with a commentary and a set of questions for reflection and discussion. The focus of the May 1982 reflection was on Christian unity, a fundamental theme of the MJCI. A translation follows:

Christian Unity (Eph. 4:1-6)

Introduction: Ephesians is the epistle of Christian unity—the unity of the universal church, not of particular communities. In Ephesians there is one predominant theme: the eternal will and plan of God to create a single community of all persons in Christ. In the salutation (1:2) we hear the word *Peace*—the greeting extended to all. This word appears seven times in Ephesians, more than in any other epistle except Romans. It announces a basic theme—the unity and harmony of all persons in Christ. Chapters 4 to 6 are practical applications to the Christian life.

Commentary:

Verse 1. Those who have been called to participate in this important ministry must live in accordance with their calling.

Verse 2. IN ALL HUMILITY: In Greek literature, humility is not a virtue; on the contrary, it signifies a lack of spirit. Christ, however, elevated service to others to the rank of virtue, offering his own life as an example. IN PATIENCE: the renunciation of vengeance.

Verse 3. GUARD THAT UNITY WHOSE SOURCE IS THE SPIRIT: The Spirit is the unique, interior source of the Christian life and, as such, continually impels all members of the Body toward that which secures peace and harmony.

Verse 4. ONLY ONE BODY: One, single, external, visible community. ONLY ONE SPIRIT: Only one interior source. ONLY ONE HOPE: The Spirit is the pledge or promise of the future, unified community (1:14).

Verse 5. ONLY ONE LORD: Christians promise obedience to one Lord alone in their profession of faith (Rom. 10:9). ONLY ONE FAITH: The relationship of this epistle to the pastoral epistles makes it possible to see that "faith" here signifies a body of doctrine (Tim. 3:9, 6:21). ONLY ONE BAPTISM: In 1 Corinthians 1:10-18, Paul alludes to the fact that Christians have been "submerged" in the same Christ through baptism as proof that there should be no division in the community because of allegiance to some personal leaders (Gal. 3:27).

Verse 6. ONLY ONE GOD AND PARENT OF ALL: All persons are united as brothers and sisters, children of the same Parent.

Conclusion. It is the will of God that we be united in the bond of

PEACE: the union and harmony of all persons in Christ. The absolutely fundamental reason for this is mentioned in verses 5 and 6 of chapter 4: We have ONLY ONE LORD, ONE FAITH, ONE BAPTISM, ONE GOD AND FATHER OF ALL.

Questions for Reflection:

1. What are the main barriers that impede our unity? Enumerate them.
2. Which of these barriers are real and difficult to overcome?
3. If the Spirit is the unique interior source of the Christian life, what is our commitment and responsibility in working for the unity of the church?

It is clear from this reflection that the leaders of the MJCI place great importance on scriptural reflection. It is an integral part of every one of their meetings. It is what they are promoting for young Nicaraguans actively involved in the process of national reconstruction. Consequently, in any pairing relationship with North American groups, they ask that such groups be sure to include their own faith reflections on their activities for justice and peace, and solidarity, in their communications with the MJCI leadership.

Because of its independence from CEPAD, the MJCI leadership looks for funding from solidarity groups and churches in North America and Europe. It intends to keep in existence and has worked out a 3-year plan for doing so. It invites North American churches and especially youth groups to consider pairing with it. One North American group—a campus ministry program at Eastern Oklahoma State University—has begun a pairing relationship with MJCI and others are possible. To explore this possibility and for further information about MJCI or a copy of the 3-year plan, write to Luis Adonis Niño, Secretario General, MJCI, Apartado 5907, Managua, Nicaragua. The complete telephone number from the U.S.A. is 011-505-2-31754.

APPENDIX

ORD (Organization of Disabled Revolutionaries) was founded in 1980 by a group of disabled persons who met each other while receiving treatment at a rehabilitation center in Managua. Because they had only recently suffered their disabilities, they were very conscious of the enormous psychological and social obstacles that they would have to overcome in their fight for a full and productive life. On finding out about the kinds of services, equipment, and orientation available to them and others with physical, audiovisual, and other sensorial limitations, these disabled persons concluded that there was a serious lack of services for the disabled and of educational literature for the general public imbued with erroneous concepts about the needs and potential abilities of the disabled. For these reasons, the group worked to form ORD.

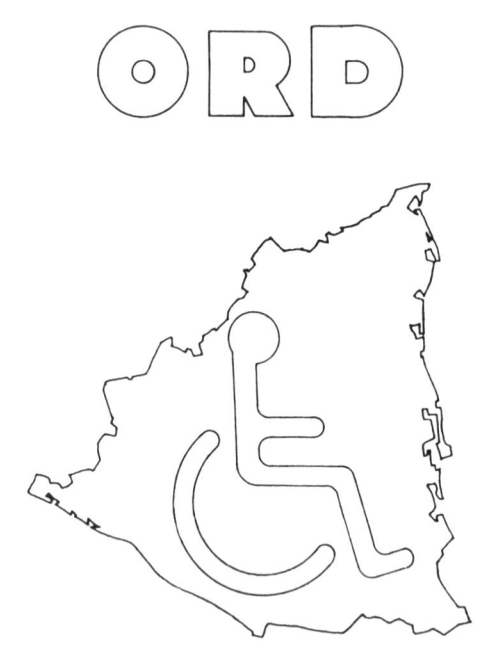

The principle goal of ORD is to promote the progressive integration of the disabled into the economic, social, and political life of the new Nicaragua. In order to achieve this goal, ORD has developed a twofold strategy:

1. To help disabled persons reconstruct their self-worth and confidence, and to develop their skills and independence.

2. To make society more conscious of and responsive to the problems and needs of the disabled.

The activities of ORD are concentrated on seven target areas:

1. *Transportation.* ORD has developed a campaign of conscientization of taxi-driver cooperatives to improve the transportation of the disabled.

2. *Architectural barriers.* ORD has developed a program to make workplaces, public buildings, study centers, hospitals, parks, recreation centers, and the like, accessible to the handicapped.

3. *Massive conscientization of society.* ORD has developed a campaign to conscientize society vis-à-vis the disabled through discussions in local communities, work places, schools, and so forth.

4. *New laws.* ORD, in conjunction with other organizations, is working to introduce laws that will protect the rights of the disabled.

5. *Instruction of the disabled.* ORD instructs disabled persons —through discussions, movies, pamphlets, and other means—on the themes of independence, self-care, and the like.

6. *Centralized organization.* ORD attempts to organize all disabled persons and introduce them to a single campaign plan for their rights.

7. *Integration into sports.* In cooperation with other organizations, ORD is encouraging the participation of disabled persons in sports.

CHAPTER FOUR

Witness for Peace: Solidarity Political Action

In July 1983, 156 North Americans traveled to Jalapa on the Nicaraguan-Honduran border for what they called an International Peace Vigil. Because of the positive response from Nicaraguans and because there seemed to be a lessening of hostilities in the area when these North Americans were present, the idea of a continuous nonviolent presence was born. A national Witness for Peace (WFP) Steering Committee was created in October. It issued the following statement of purpose:

> To develop an ever-broadening, prayerful, biblically-based community of U.S. citizens who stand with the Nicaraguan people by acting in continuous nonviolent resistance to U.S. overt or covert intervention in their country; to mobilize public opinion and help change U.S. foreign policy to one which fosters justice, peace, and friendship; and to welcome others in this endeavor who vary in spiritual approach but who are one with us in purpose.

The WFP presence in Nicaragua takes two forms: a long-term team and short-term delegations. The long-term team has a twofold assignment. First, the team maintains a continuous presence among the people by engaging in village life and work in Jalapa, and now in other zones of conflict in Nicaragua, investigating and reporting on "contra" incursions and attacks. Secondly, the team hosts and orients the short-term delegations who visit conflict zones. The long-termers are fluent in Spanish and make a 6-month commitment. Short-term delegations are organized state by state throughout the U.S.A. and spend two weeks in Nicaragua, one of which is in a conflict zone. Every month in 1984, at least two short-term teams (from ten to twenty persons in each team) traveled to Nicaragua. Members of these delegations are persons from all walks of life, few of whom have previously been to Nicaragua but all of whom are opposed to the idea that their tax dollars should be used to fund international terrorism against the civilian population of Nicaragua. The delegations work and worship with Nicaraguans in conflict zones and also learn about the Nicaraguan socio-political process, particularly the more controversial issues highlighted in the U.S. press.

WFP is building a grassroots network of concerned U.S. citizens. The commitment to change U.S. policy begins before joining a short-term delegation and continues after returning home. Each participant shares and shapes WFP by the following covenant:

1. We commit ourselves to a prayerful, biblical approach and unity with one another as the foundation for this project.

2. We commit ourselves to nonviolence in word and deed as the essential operating principle for the WFP.

3. We commit ourselves to honesty and openness in our relationships with one another.

4. We commit ourselves to maintaining the political independence of the WFP.

5. We commit ourselves to act in solidarity and community with the Nicaraguan people, respecting their lives, their culture, and their decisions. We will respect the guidelines worked out with the Nicaraguan government in regard to our presence and mobility in the border area.

6. We commit significant time and financial resources on a regular basis to the WFP.

JALAPA

I hope that the following personal reflections on my own WFP participation after Christmas 1983 will make the various dimensions and goals of WFP more concrete. They may also provide a glimpse of how the war is affecting the people and of what the Nicaraguan Revolution looks like in a rural area.

Nonviolent Presence

The first dimension of the WFP effort is to provide a nonviolent presence in the midst of war. In the case of Jalapa, this means going to the Nicaraguan-Honduran border to a village called Teotecacinte. It is here that the "contras" have crossed over into Nicaragua numerous times, have destroyed much of the village and crops, and have continued to shell the community from their sanctuaries in Honduras. So it is here that WFP teams go to stand and pray—on the edge of a tobacco field only 300 yards from the border.

One of the members of our delegation, Fr. Dennis Kennedy, reflected on his experience:

Two young students, militiamen, Miguel and Guillermo, were our guides. Miguel is a teacher when he is not in the service, and Guillermo is studying ornithology. They showed us, as we walked along toward the border, the fences and houses shredded by mortar shrapnel. We heard of the woman during the attack who had headed for the shelter only to look back and see her young daughter's body lying in the street. She ran back, grabbed her hand, and dragged her toward the shelter. When she arrived, she saw that her daughter had been decapitated by a shell. She then braved fire to go back and get the lost head so the body could be buried intact.

We saw many more "defenses" here—ditches, one or two underground shelters of wood and dirt. We cautiously made our way to the border to pray, all of us rather frightened. We reached a newly-planted tobacco field and began to cross it slowly in two small groups. We were told that we were certainly under the eyes of the "contras" about 300 yards away in Honduras and we then laid down our small crash packs and unfurled our large banner painted with figures of persons standing hand-in-hand with the words *"acción permanente cristiana por la paz*—Witness for Peace" around it. We prayed for about half an hour. At one point, Miguel and Guillermo took off their rifles and gunbelts, and joined us at the banner, which really buoyed our spirits. However, it was a very dangerous thing for them to do. After a while, we folded up the banner and headed back into town, sobered and exhilarated at the same time.

Standing with the People

The second dimension of the WFP witness is to stand in solidarity with the people of Nicaragua. This means a variety of things. Just walking the dirt streets of Jalapa, which has swelled because of the war from 8,000 to 12,000 persons, provided many opportunities to engage in conversation with the people. Visiting the home of 44-year-old Esperanza on a Saturday afternoon as she and several of her children and a neighbor were baking rolls and bread in their front-room brick oven turned out to be a special experience. After chatting for a while, the three of us promised to return later to buy some of her rolls. "Later" turned out to be the next morning and all the rolls were gone. Quickly she left the small front room of her three-room house and returned with a tray of a dozen or so rolls. She insisted we take them and she refused our offers to pay for them.

As a small token of thanks and solidarity, I gave her the solidarity button ("Stop U.S. intervention in Nicaragua") I was wearing. It was obvious that she regarded the button as a special gift. She showed it to her elderly mother and began to talk about her family at length. The children joined in the conversation, one having just returned from militia duty in the mountains. We experienced a special closeness in those moments, despite some language barriers.

Another chance meeting occurred earlier that Saturday morning. Two of us wandered into a corner store that had an ENABAS sign over the door (the government agency that supervises the distribution of basic goods). We introduced ourselves to Lucil, the manager, and began asking about the availability of supplies. We had heard of widespread shortages throughout the country—flour, rice, beans, soap, cooking oil, milk, sugar. According to Lucil, Jalapa was not yet experiencing serious shortages in these supplies. Later we learned that the government is trying to ensure that border towns such as Jalapa be as amply supplied as possible, because of efforts by the "contras" to entice Nicaraguans into Honduras by the promise of a better life. Four hundred dollars was the amount, according to Jalapa leaders, being offered to Nicaraguans who would move to Honduras.

Someone else described how planes from Honduras dropped toys along the border areas of Nicaragua on La Purísima (December 8th, the biggest feast day of the year), promising additional toys to children who would come to Honduras.

Despite government efforts, extensive volunteer campaigns to harvest crops, and donations from around the world, shortages are spreading because of economic sabotage by the "contras" and the CIA. By May 1984 these shortages had spread to Jalapa where the entire community was without cooking oil for a week. In less strategic areas of the countryside, shortages are more acute. *Campesinos* who had received basic medicines for the first time, as a result of the Revolution, are now having to go without them again.

Esperanza (left) with her family

As a small token of thanks and solidarity, I gave Esperanza the solidarity button I was wearing. It was obvious that she regarded it as a special gift.

Standing with the people of Jalapa also meant listening to the stories of those victimized by the war even more directly, especially those who had lost spouses or children. A very special group of Nicaraguans are the *Madres de los Héroes y Mártires* ("mothers of the heroes and martyrs"). We were privileged to get to meet and listen to several of them.

One evening two of them, both named María, shared their stories. One's son had been killed in August 1983; the other's son on June 18, 1979 (during the final insurrection against Somoza).

Both mothers spoke passionately and simply about the ordinariness of their sons: "They were no great leaders, just young persons who could no longer stand the poverty and repression under Somoza." They concluded with an eloquent expression of their Christian faith: "This is our way of living out the demands of our Christian faith—to lay down our lives for our sisters and brothers, as Jesus said." And then after a pause, "And to forgive those who have killed our sons." From the serenity of their faces and the softness yet strength of their voices, it seemed clear that they had done what they said—they had forgiven their enemies.

Walking the streets of Jalapa provided other opportunities to stand with the victims of the war. Two of us chanced upon the Jalapa hospital where we talked with a nurse outside the compound. After giving us some basic information—the hospital had twenty-eight beds and was served by six doctors and sixteen nurses, treating civilians as well as military personnel—she invited us into the ward where two wounded combatants were lying in bed. I sat with one who had been wounded just the day before. Several tubes were supplying life-sustaining fluids and the medical team surrounding him shared their doubts that he would live. This was not just another statistic, "war casualty #1,000" for that year. This was 18-year-old José Taleno, who was lapsing in and out of consciousness. With my hand on his leg in a gesture of solidarity, I raged inside, vowed to tell his story and name to North Americans, and became more determined than ever to challenge a U.S. policy that has this as its consequence.

Praying with the People

My determination was further strengthened by another moving incident only a few hours later. The third dimension of the WFP witness is to pray with the people. It was New Year's Eve about 8 P.M. when we got word that a family wanted us to come and pray with them. Their 16-year-old son had just been killed (one of seven whose bodies had been brought to Jalapa that day). As we entered the home of Lorenzo Osorios, dozens of persons and a military honor guard surrounded his son's casket in their small living room. More than a hundred others gathered outside the home. We read the "World Peace Prayer" in Spanish with the family and embraced Lorenzo and his wife.

Then the 80-year-old veteran, Lorenzo, in his uniform and with his old rifle over his shoulder (we learned later that he had fought with Sandino against the U.S. marines more than fifty years earlier), addressed us: "This is the second son we have lost this year. It is hard to accept the Cross. We all have to learn patience. But Jesus walked this path before us." Such a depth of faith we experienced in this people, a people so well acquainted with the "death" dimension of the paschal mystery, the "death and resurrection" core of our Christian faith!

Working with the People

The fourth dimension of the WFP effort is to work side by side with the people. For some WFP teams, this has meant reconstruction work after "contra" attacks or working in refugee camps. For us, it meant working in the harvests. So many workers have had to spend their time in the popular militia defending their country that there has been a real shortage of workers to harvest the crops so vital to the national economy. The day we arrived in Jalapa we encountered a group of about one hundred high-school students who were just returning from two weeks in the coffee harvest. They had sacrificed their Christmas vacation.

Our day in the fields was Monday, the day that at least seventy-five members of the local Assembly of God volunteer each week to harvest the crops. Although they are not willing to take up arms to defend the country and although many members of the more fundamentalist Protestant churches in Nicaragua have not been supportive of the revolutionary process, these members have been very willing to share in it through their volunteer work.

As we were waiting for the trucks to transport us to the fields, a volunteer named Alfonso was willing to put up with our very imperfect Spanish and talk with us about his life. He was a farm worker who had moved with his family to Jalapa from an outlying village because of repeated "contra" attacks. The 120 or more villages in the mountains around Jalapa have been forced by the war to consolidate into some twenty larger communities— some of which are refugee camps. These attacks focus not on military targets but on economic destruction ($128 million was the estimated loss from such attacks in 1983) and terrorism (in the form of kidnapping, rape, torture, mutilation of bodies to prevent burials). Only several weeks earlier, an agricultural cooperative not far from Jalapa had been the target—fourteen persons killed, homes destroyed, and crops burned. Alfonso told us how his life had changed since the Revolution. His wage as a farm worker had jumped from 10 or 15 córdobas a day ($1.00-$1.50 at the 10-to-1 exchange rate; 30¢-40¢ at the 28-to-1 rate) to 40 córdobas a day. "There is no more repression," he added. "And now the land belongs to the people."

The day together in the fields was a real solidarity experience. The eight Nicaraguans to whose work team three of us were assigned were willing to joke and sing with us as well as engage us in more serious conversation. Later that day as the eleven of us waited for the trucks to take us back to Jalapa, we encountered a group of young militia members. Twenty-year-old Tomás was their leader. At age 11, he had joined the FSLN and the struggle against Somoza, in the mountains around Ocotal and Estelí (to the south of Jalapa). He was 16 at the time of the 1979 triumph. Since then he had been in the militia—and studying and teaching economics at UPOLI, the polytechnic college in Managua. We had a hard time believing he could be teaching at the college level, especially when being an officer in the militia meant that he alternated a full year of active duty with a year to pursue his civilian career. Subsequently we learned that most other militia members serve in their home area and work or study during the day and do *vigilancia* (patrol) at night and are always "on call" for duty should a military crisis emerge. Such a crisis generally has meant being activated from four days to two weeks. We also learned that Tomás may well have been a college teacher because of the intense economic and political study demanded by the FSLN of all its members during the years of struggle against Somoza.

Nonviolent Protest

The fifth dimension of the WFP effort is nonviolent protest against U.S. intervention in Nicaragua. For WFP members in Nicaragua, this means joining the weekly vigil in front of the U.S. embassy in Managua. But more importantly, it means ongoing public education and political action upon return to the U.S.A. Both before and after the trip, letters and visits to legislators, press conferences and interviews for television and radio shows, as well as presentations to church and community groups are important aspects of this work. In the case of the St. Louisans who were part of the post-Christmas delegation, not all the media coverage generated was supportive, as the following editorial from the St. Louis *Globe-Democrat* indicates:

Lindell Boulevard's Foreign Agents

Who, exactly, are members of the St. Louis Inter-Faith Committee on Latin America, what is their purpose, and where do they get money to send Sandinista sympathizers on junkets to Communist-controlled Nicaragua?

These are questions members of St. Louis churches might well be asking their religious leaders.

St. Louisans again have been exposed to the spectacle of a "Witness for Peace" delegation returning from Nicaragua and spouting pro-Sandinistas, anti-U.S. statements.

Included in the group were James McGinnis, director of the so-called Institute for Peace and Justice, a Catholic priest who teaches at Kenrick Seminary, and three nuns.

They held a press conference at their Lindell Boulevard headquarters on the very day Americans were outraged over the death of an Army helicopter pilot who was downed and then killed by gunfire from Nicaraguan forces even though his craft landed inside Honduras.

Despite well-documented accounts of religious persecution and human rights violations in Nicaragua, McGinnis and his traveling companions call reports that are supportive of the U.S. a "myth" and a "big lie."

In a prepared "Report from Nicaragua," McGinnis proudly states that "Witness of Peace teams come to stand in solidarity with the people, these victims of U.S. policy; to stand at the border and face those implementing U.S. policy."

According to McGinnis, "The evil represented in U.S. policy in Central America as well as U.S. escalation of the nuclear arms race threatens the moral fibre of our nation. Our very soul as a people is at stake."

A much better authority on Nicaragua and on the state of

people's souls is Bishop Salvador Schlaefer, an American Catholic missionary who at Christmastime accompanied 1,300 Miskito Indians into Honduras from Nicaragua, where they were being persecuted by the Sandinistas.

Nicaraguan air force planes and soldiers pursued the refugees and shot at them enroute, Bishop Schlaefer said. The Sandinistas had falsely reported Bishop Schlaefer was killed resisting freedom fighters.

McGinnis and his associates consider the freedom fighters, known as "contras," as enemies of the Nicaraguan people. That's like making George Washington the bad guy and King George III the good guy in the American Revolution.

If the Inter-Faith Committee on Latin America continues as a center for Communist Sandinista propaganda, its members ought to register with the State Department as foreign agents [*Globe Democrat*, Jan. 14, 1984].

The "freedom-fighters," as the editorial describes the "contras," are anything but freedom-fighters. Part of the WFP effort of public education and political action is the documentation of massacres and other consequences of U.S. policy in Nicaragua—to tell the (often gruesome) truth about U.S. policy. A monthly WFP *Newsbrief* provides documentation.

The following account of a "contra" attack on the village of Waslala and neighboring villages in central Nicaragua is taken from the June 1984 *Newsbrief* and answers the *Globe-Democrat* characterization of the "contras" as modern-day George Washingtons. Because such a characterization is used by Reagan administration representatives to generate support for aid to the "contras," duplicating this report (and others) and sending it to legislators and to editors of newspapers and other opinion makers is an important political action:

The Attack on the Town of Waslala

[On April 26th, Douglas Spence and Jean Abbott, long-term Witness for Peace volunteers, travelled to the town of Waslala to investigate and report on the contra attacks in early April against this town. They spent four days in the town and surrounding vil-

lages and met many people from whom they compiled the following information.]

The small town of Waslala sits along the Waslala River and the dirt highway which connects the western city of Matagalpa with the Nicaraguan Atlantic coast. As a strategic geographical point in north-central Nicaragua, this town suffered an attack by nearly 1800 contra troops beginning on 3 April 1984.

CONTRA OBJECTIVE

According to a local security official the contra objective was to take the town of Waslala and to declare a "liberated" territory from which to send a call for direct international military assistance.

"The contras attempted to cut off Waslala from the rest of the country," he said. "They cut down telephone and electricity poles leading into Waslala, destroyed the bridge between Waslala and the eastern town of Siuna (at El Guabo), and they tried, unsuccessfully, to destroy the bridge on the Yaosca River, between Waslala and Matagalpa to the west."

MAJOR ATTACK

One contra column attacked army outposts on the northern edge of town, in the Claudia Chamorro neighborhood, taking and using civilian homes as positions from which to launch mortars, small rockets, and automatic weapons fire. According to local soldiers and civilians about 350 contras engaged this sector of town during the seven-hour April 3 battle.

On the western edge of town, near the Waslala River, the local hospital appeared to be another tactical objective. According to the hospital director, Dr. Dina Rodia, 29, three mortar rounds came very close to the hospital buildings. Nearly 350 contras tried to cross the river to capture the hospital site, but they were repelled.

The third point of attack was the large hill, El Papayo, the site of an earlier truck ambush, on the eastern edge of town. A local militia member who participated in the defense of El Papayo said that about 200 contras fought during the seven-hour battle to gain the high ground but were driven off.

CIVILIANS TERRIFIED

Civilians in the neighborhoods under attack were terrified. Mrs. María Castilla Piñeda, 72, who lives on the edge of town in the Claudia Chamorro neighborhood, said, "When the battle began, I threw myself on the floor of my bedroom. A large band of contras came right up behind my house and began to fire at the town with all those big weapons. Bullets were flying all over the place. I could smell the gun powder. Some shrapnel came into the house," she said, pointing out the holes in her wooden house.

CONTRAS TORTURE AND MURDER VOLUNTEER POLICEMAN

Mr. Teófilo Mejía, 24, a local small-scale farmer who served the community as a member of the volunteer police association, was eating breakfast with his wife, María Rivera Amadro de Mejía, and their four children. Mrs. Mejía managed a small bakery out of their home.

"When we heard the first mortar shots by the contras, we all took refuge in our bomb shelter," said Mrs. Mejía. "About 300 to 400 contras came up the small rise to our house. After searching through all our belongings, they came and pulled us out of the bomb shelter. When they found my husband's volunteer police uniform they began to beat him up and said they were going to kill us all."

Mr. Mejía got on his knees and pleaded with the contras that they let his wife and children go free. "My husband said they could do what they planned with him, but to show mercy for the women and children. So they let us go—but, as we fled into the woods, they threw a grenade at us. It wounded me slightly on the shoulder, but, thank God, none of the children were hurt.

"Then, as we hid in the woods, we could hear my husband scream and we knew they were torturing him. About 12:30 P.M. we heard an explosion. We saw smoke rising and knew that they had torched our house.

"About an hour later, as the contras were retreating, they stopped at my mother's house (which is located one-quarter mile from the Mejía farm) and kidnapped my two younger brothers, José Antonio, 13, and Emilio Ubaldo, 14, as well as my sister, Reina Riveras Amador, 16. Neither my parents nor brothers nor sister were involved in any popular organization or in politics.

They were kidnapped 22 days ago and we have not heard of them since.

"After the contras left the area," Mrs. Mejía continued, "we went to our house to find my husband. We found him lying in front of our totally burned house. They had cut his arms with a knife and had completely smashed in his head until it was not recognizable. They used a big knife to cut a large cross in his back," she said with a trembling voice.

María, while strong in spirit, was grieved over her loss and at reliving the tragedy for this report. She wept softly and spoke of her four fatherless children: "The five-year-old asked for some money to go to the drug store to buy some medicine to bring back his daddy." Then after a few minutes of silence she said, "All I ask is that you pray for us."

FAILED OBJECTIVE

In the Claudia Chamorro neighborhood, after the contras came within 200 yards of the town's defensive positions, their leader, El Yankee, was killed in combat. While an accurate count of contra casualties was not readily available, at least nine deaths were counted. The local militia and army personnel suffered 18 killed and about 15 wounded. According to local parish records, funeral masses were held for 30 civilians from Waslala and the surrounding villages—all victims of the contra attack and violence.

FRUSTRATED CONTRA RAIDERS TERRORIZE VILLAGE

El Achiote, a small farm village located three hours by footpath from Waslala, faced a contra occupation of 300 troops on the afternoon of April 1st. "They took my two grandchildren, Gregoria Martínez, 16, and Teodoro Pérez, 13, and tortured them and cut their throats. We found their bodies with many torture marks all over them," said Julia Paiz.

Another woman, age 20 (who requested anonymity due to her fear of reprisals from the contras), reported that her husband, 25, was captured the same day as Mrs. Piaz' grandchildren. The three were cousins. He was bound with a rope and led to a grove of trees where he saw that his cousins had already been killed. "My husband told me that they beat him, punched him in the chest with knives, and cut his arms and fingers with sharp rocks.

He held his breath so that the contras thought he was dead. Then they left him."

When the local villagers learned of these murders many fled into the mountains for safety. Mrs. Antonia Gómez Hernández, 45, who is a mother of six children, told us, "We were afraid, so we hid in the deep forest. The contras had come and threatened us many times before this and this time we knew they were going to carry out those threats. We took our children and a little food and we hid."

The contras left El Achiote the evening of April 2nd in the direction of Waslala, where the battle described above commenced at 6:30 A.M. on April 3rd.

Having been driven off by Nicaraguan army and militia units, the contras retreated into the mountains, again passing through El Achiote village. In a rage of frustration and destruction, they pulled 19 civilians out of their homes and shot them on the spot. Then the contras burned down 11 houses in the village square, the school house, and the kitchen behind the village chapel. Considering themselves the "defenders of religion," they did not burn the chapel itself.

"By April 5th," Mrs. Hernández continued, "we were hungry from hiding in the forest. We estimated that the contras had by now travelled far north toward Honduras, so we came out of hiding. We now live in the safety of the town of Waslala."

CONTRAS BURN SCHOOLS

In the course of the attack on the area surrounding Waslala, the contras burned three village schools to the ground. All these schools, the only centers for education in the remote rural communities, were constructed since the 1979 triumph over the dictator, Anastasio Somoza.

In addition to the events in El Achiote, the villages of El Guabo and Kubali suffered the burning of houses, kidnappings, and murders by the contra terrorists. In El Guabo, the Rodolfo Amador Gallegos school was totally burned.

"Now the children don't have any place to study. The teachers are afraid to stay in the village now," lamented one mother (who spoke on the condition that her name not be used due to her fear of reprisals if the contras return). "We received the construction materials from international friends and we of this community organized our volunteer work crews to build the school house," she added. The school in El Guabo was constructed in 1982 with material provided by the European Economic Community (EEC). This organization is also known as the European Common Market and most of its member nations are also members of the NATO alliance with the U.S.

WFP PROJECTS IN THE U.S.A.

The public education and political action dimension of WFP has taken other forms as well. On October 13, 1984, a series of "citizen hearings" were conducted in more than a dozen U.S. communities. At each hearing, written and photographic evidence of attacks on Nicaragua and the human costs of U.S. intervention were presented to local congresspersons as well as the general public. WFP pamphlets summarizing this evidence are available for sharing with political representatives, opinion makers, and friends—as part of our ongoing public education and political action work.

Finally and even more dramatically, the prospect of a possible invasion of Nicaragua involving U.S. troops led WFP and a number of other U.S. religious peace and justice groups to formulate a contingency plan to deter or counter such an invasion. This plan, which Jim Wallis wrote of in detail in the August 1984 issue of *Sojourners* magazine, under the title "A Pledge of Resistance" (see below), was announced in the fall of 1984 to the press and the U.S. government in the hope that a promise of resistance on such a large scale would help deter the possibility of U.S. invasion. Discussions also began about how this or similar plans could be useful in opposing U.S. military escalation elsewhere in Central America.

A Pledge of Resistance

*A contingency plan
in the event of a U.S. invasion of Nicaragua*

BACKGROUND

The plan began to emerge during a retreat. On November 2 to 4, 1983, representatives of the Christian peace movement met at the Kirkridge retreat center in northeastern Pennsylvania for Bible study, prayer, and political discernment. The Kirkridge retreat has become an annual event drawing together those from major denominations and churches, religious orders, national organizations, communities, campaigns, and local action groups that are providing leadership for peacemaking in the churches.

We met in the aftermath of the Grenada invasion. Some of us were in frequent contact with Nicaraguan churchpeople who were expressing great fear that their country would also be invaded. Our deep concern and friendship with Nicaraguan brothers and sisters set the tone for our prayer and discussion.

Witness for Peace, a grassroots effort to keep a continuous, nonviolent presence of U.S. Christians in Nicaragua's war zones, was to be publicly launched in December and was already attracting a great deal of support and enthusiasm. We all committed ourselves to that bold initiative and together drew up a statement pledging ourselves to a plan of action in the event of a United States invasion of Nicaragua (see "A Promise of Resistance," *Sojourners*, December 1983). That "contingency plan" was subsequently presented to each of our constituencies in the churches and sent to every member of Congress, to the Departments of State and Defense, to the CIA, and to the president, informing them of our intentions should they undertake direct military action against Nicaragua.

Witness for Peace has now become a strong, grassroots movement involving thousands of U.S. citizens from the churches, religious community, and beyond in direct, nonviolent opposition to the CIA's not-so-secret "covert" war against Nicaragua. Meanwhile the contingency plan has undergone more discussion and refinement. Conversations have taken place within Witness for Peace, with the Inter-Religious Task Force on Central America, among the Christian peace groups that planned the Kirkridge retreat, in local church, peace, and action groups across the country, and with many churchpeople and groups in Nicaragua, including North Americans who live and work there.

The response has been enormously positive, and feedback has shaped the evolving plan. As people and groups have heard of the plan, they have enthusiastically committed themselves to it. At the national level, a number of groups are now involved: Witness for Peace, the Inter-Religious Task Force on Central America,

Southern Christian Leadership Conference, Fellowship of Reconciliation, Pax Christi, New Call to Peacemaking, World Peacemakers, Clergy and Laity Concerned, American Friends Service Committee, SANE, and Sojourners. Church and denominational networks are also rapidly becoming involved.

We all believe, along with friends in Nicaragua, that it is time to concretize the contingency plan and be ready to implement it as soon as possible.

PURPOSE

We hope either to prevent a direct U.S. invasion of Nicaragua or to make such military action so politically costly it will have to be halted. By announcing a credible and coordinated plan of massive public resistance, we hope to forestall an expanded war against Nicaragua. If the U.S. military undertakes direct action against Nicaragua, we will undertake nonviolent direct action against it on the largest scale possible. In so doing we hope to bring the issue before the American people, pressure Congress to act, and demand an immediate end to the invasion and the withdrawal of U.S. forces from Nicaragua.

THE PLAN

In the event of a U.S. invasion of Nicaragua, the following will happen:

1. A signal for action will go out to regional, state, and local contact people and groups.

2. People across the country will gather at a previously designated church in their local community (at least one in every congressional district). These churches will be the gathering points for receiving and sharing information, for prayer and mutual support, for preparing and commissioning one another for action.

3. A nonviolent vigil will be established at the congressional field offices of each U.S. senator and representative. Each office will be peacefully occupied until that congressperson votes to end the invasion.

4. A large number of people will come to Washington, D.C. (in delegations from every area of the country) to engage in nonviolent civil disobedience at the White House to demand an end to the invasion.

5. The United States citizens in Nicaragua who are in active

partnership with us (Witness for Peace, Maryknoll, the Committee of U.S. Citizens in Nicaragua, etc.) will launch their own plan of action in Nicaragua in concert with us. Depending on the political situation, the timing of the invasion, and the possibility of getting into Nicaragua before or during an invasion, we will send other people to Nicaragua to join in the actions of the United States citizens already there, if our partners in Nicaragua feel such an action would be advisable.

IMPLEMENTATION

The contingency plan will be carried out by a number of local groups acting together (the local networks, chapters, and contacts of the supporting national organizations and other local groups). In each local area, an ad hoc committee should be created to formulate and carry out the plan locally. The following activities will be the responsibility of the local committees:

1. Designating the churches in each local area where people will gather.

2. Planning a service of prayer, preparation, and commissioning for action.

3. Establishing a local scenario for action, consistent with the national plan, in each congressional district.

4. Carrying out the preparations and training necessary for each local action.

5. Selecting a delegation to go to Washington, D.C., for civil disobedience.

6. Gathering pledges from the largest possible number of people in each local area who will commit themselves to act in the event of a U.S. invasion of Nicaragua. The list of those pledged to action will stay at the local level, but the number of those pledged to action will be sent to Washington to announce to the government and to the press.

COMMUNICATION

Witness for Peace regional offices have agreed to serve as contact points for the communication system of the contingency plan. When they receive information or signals for action, they will pass the word on to contingency plan state coordinators, who will then contact local coordinators. The Witness for Peace regional coordinators will also help to facilitate establishment of the communication network in each of the regions. The Witness for Peace regional coordinators are listed below.

West Coast: Mary Kurt-Mason, 515 Broadway, Santa Cruz, CA 95060; (408) 425-3733. **Southwest:** Buddy Summers or Lynn Holmes, 4220 S.P.I.D. #212, Corpus Christi, TX 78411; (512) 852-8755. **Northern Midwest:** Betty Wolcott, 3221 S. Lake Dr., Milwaukee, WI 53207; (414) 744-1160. **Central Midwest:** Grace Gyori, 3913 N. St. Louis, Chicago, IL 60618; (312) 267-7881. **New England:** Bob Bonthius or Fran Truitt, RD 2, Box 422A, Ellsworth, ME 04605; (207) 422-9007. **Mid Atlantic:** John Collins or Bill Webber, 198 Broadway, New York 10038; (212) 964-6730. **Southeast:** Betsy Crites or Josefina Tiryakian, 1414 Woodland Dr., Durham, NC 27701; (919) 688-5400.

Because of both regular contact with Nicaragua and proximity to Washington decision-making and press, the Witness for Peace Washington office and Sojourners have agreed to be the points from which information and the signal for action will be given. A consultative process of decision-making involving others is being established to decide when the signal for action should be given. This U.S. contingency plan is being coordinated with the plans being developed by our U.S. friends in Nicaragua, who will determine the feasibility and advisability of more U.S. citizens joining them in Nicaragua in the event of an invasion.

CONCLUSION

Given the urgent situation in Nicaragua and the possibilities of further United States escalation, the contingency plan should be ready for implementation as soon as possible. This call will go out from the various organizations, groups, and constituencies involved. The contingency plan will subsequently be announced to the government and to the press in the hope that a pledge of resistance on such a large scale will help deter the possibility of a United States invasion. Discussions are under way about how this or similar plans might be useful in opposing U.S. military escalation elsewhere in Central America.

The work on this effort has already brought people and groups together. We all hope that will continue. To succeed, the plan needs a broad base of support. Making this promise of resistance and doing the work to make the promise credible will surely deepen our understanding and experience of the things that make for peace. If the armies of the United States are mobilized to wage war on Nicaragua, may a mighty nonviolent army of U.S. citizens also be mobilized to wage peace.

Such mass mobilization of individuals and groups at the local level requires the establishment of what is sometimes known as an "urgent action network"—essentially a mechanism for disseminating information and getting something done quickly. In St. Louis, it was the local WFP taskforce (of the Inter-Faith Committee on Latin America) that took responsibility for setting up a citywide network. This process includes six steps:

1. Identify the groups to be contacted: peace and justice groups; religious communities; schools, especially seminaries and college campus ministry groups; professional associations with social concerns (lawyers, social workers, etc.); church agencies and some social service agencies.

2. Arrange these groups in some kind of "telephone-tree" order, each group being responsible for contacting a limited number of other groups, with the more responsive/involved groups higher on the list. Contact these groups to see which ones are actually willing to be part of the network.

3. Ask each group to set up its own *internal* telephone-tree/urgent action network, so that its individual members can be contacted personally. This may be a more elaborate and difficult task because of the number of members involved. In the case of the Institute for Peace and Justice, for instance, with some five hundred "shareholders," 80 percent of whom are in the St. Louis area, the "urgent action network" mechanism began with a mailing to every shareholder. In that mailing was included a 4-page analysis/action piece concerning U.S. policy toward Nicaragua in light of the invasion of Grenada, and an invitation to join an urgent action network focusing on one or more issue areas. The agenda of the Institute was broader than Central America, and it wanted to use this opportunity to enable it to respond more effectively to its other issue priorities as well.

4. Designate one group or person or a small group of represent-

atives of several groups to be responsible for deciding what kinds of events will activate the telephone-tree and for actually activating it.

5. Identify the specific actions that persons will be invited to do in the event of an invasion.

6. Test the telephone-tree, perhaps giving participating groups several weeks to set up their own internal telephone-trees.

This whole nonviolent direct action campaign of which these local urgent action networks are a part represents in a very real sense, according to Yvonne Dilling, the Washington coordinator for WFP, "the culmination of all the Nicaraguan solidarity projects in the U.S.A. over the past couple of years." These various solidarity efforts and projects have led to an awareness of the need to confront U.S. policy in more and more dramatic and risky ways. Witness for Peace, itself the product of this growing awareness, challenges each of us to consider our own personal involvement in such a nonviolent direct action campaign and other similar actions that involve risk. But our ability and willingness to take risks on behalf of the people of Nicaragua (or any other group) is dependent on a number of internal resources (what religious writers sometimes refer to as a "spirituality" of solidarity) as well as external mechanisms. The focus of the final chapter of this book is this "inner core of solidarity"; it should be read in conjunction with this WFP chapter in particular.

For further information about specific aspects of this chapter, contact:

—the WFP national office for a subscription to the WFP *Newsbrief*. The WFP "hotline" (202-332-9230) gives current information from the different zones of conflict in Nicaragua; the hotline is updated weekly.

—Betsy Crites (1414 Woodland Dr., Durham, NC 27701; 919-688-5400) about being part of a short-term WFP delegation.

—Josefina Tiryakian (same Durham address/phone) about being part of a long-term WFP team.

—Ellie Foster (515 Broadway, Santa Cruz, CA 95060; 408-425-3733) to find out if there is a WFP support group already organized in your area.

—Sojourners (P.O. Box 29272, Washington, DC 20017; 202-636-3636) or the WFP national office for more on the nonviolent direct action campaign.

—Ron Stief (2124 Kittredge St., Suite 92, Berkeley, CA 94702; 415-848-1674) about the "citizens hearings" and pamphlets/documentation/photographs from the hearings.

CHAPTER FIVE

Children's Solidarity Projects

"SOLIDARITY PARKS" FOR JALAPA

Originally, the idea was to have North American children collect $4,000 to purchase $1 toys in Nicaragua for some 4,000 children in the northern border town of Jalapa, where WFP teams had initiated a nonviolent presence in Nicaragua. The $4,000 was collected in the St. Louis area in December 1983 and taken to Nicaragua by a WFP team on December 28, the feast of the Holy Innocents.

One of those contributing to the project was a 6-year-old boy named Tom. On Christmas Eve he gave me a bag of pennies, nickels, dimes, and quarters—all the money he had saved for two years for a special toy for himself. He told me that he had decided to give the entire $16.06 to the children of Nicaragua and asked if I would see to it that a letter he had written to the children of Nicaragua would reach them. A 13-year-old boy masterminded a caroling effort that netted $30.

When the WFP team arrived in Nicaragua, the project was changed from the purchase of toys to the construction of children's playgrounds for the three refugee centers set up near Jalapa. The reasons for the change were several: 1) toys generally do not last, whereas playgrounds do; 2) playgrounds provide many more opportunities for cooperative play than do 4,000 individual toys, and cooperation is a basic value in the new Nicaragua; 3) there were no toys to purchase in Nicaragua, a fact exploited by the "contras" as illustrated by their dropping of toys from planes along the Nicaraguan-Honduran border and promising more toys for those who would join them in Honduras.

> To Friends in Nicaragua
> I hope the war stops soon. It must be scary living where there is a war. Tom

On January 6, 1984, the $4,000 was presented to CEPAD, the Evangelical Committee for Aid and Development, for the construction of three playgrounds or "solidarity parks," as they have come to be called. Accompanying this initial gift was the following statement:

> Always we were touched by the children—their beauty, innocence, and intelligent eyes. As Witness for Peace, we came to learn about your country, to stand in solidarity with you against the destructive policies of the Reagan administration, to help in whatever way we could in productive work and to pray for peace. But this particular group, organized in the city of St. Louis, was given another task, one not directly associated with the Witness for Peace but which we are happy to carry out. It was a task given us by the children of the United States, children who wish for their

Nicaraguan brothers and sisters what children are supposed to have: laughter not tears; joy not grief; play not pain. So from the boys and girls of the United States who have no enemies here, only playmates, we present $4,000 for the construction of three playgrounds for the children of La Estancia, Escombray, and Santa Cruz. Let these solidarity parks be symbolic grounds for peace between our peoples even though, because of what they represent, they may become a focus for "contra" attack. In the face of violence, the children will play; in the face of loss, the children will sing; in spite of the war, the children will make peace.

Why Playgrounds?

In answer to the question about whether there were not more pressing needs than playgrounds, a Nicaraguan mother and leader stated: "We have had to sacrifice our children's childhood to the urgent need for national defense and cannot afford playgrounds with our own limited money, but with your help we can return some of their childhood to them." One of the monitors for the playground project reported in the summer of 1984: "Over and over, people all around Nicaragua told me what a wonderful idea they thought these playground projects were. Their children had seen such hardships and felt such terror from the war that they needed more joy and play in their lives. So many of the children have no suitable place to play. The playgrounds are an answer to a real need. The great value and love that the people have for their children would make these priority projects even in the face of so many other needs and crises the country has to deal with."

Shortages of materials due to the war delayed the beginning of the playgrounds. These shortages have been compounded by the difficulty of transporting materials. As one of the project monitors in Jalapa observed, "transportation of materials in this region is very difficult due to the lack of vehicles and very poor roads. We can certainly see the results of the naval and economic blockade glaringly here—the lack of truck and tractor spare parts and the termination of U.S. aid, some of which had been earmarked for paving the dirt road between Ocotal and Jalapa." Finally, in the fall of 1984, the first two playgrounds were completed—in La Estancia and Escombray. Funds are currently being sought to complete a third and fourth playground (an additional refugee center opened in mid-1984).

The refugee centers where the playgrounds are being located would more accurately be called resettlement projects (*asentamientos*), because they apparently will be more permanent than was thought initially. They began because persons living in the small scattered villages along the Nicaraguan-Honduran border had become the victims of continual "contra" terrorist attacks. They could not go into their fields to work without fearing that their lives would be taken or their crops burned. Consequently, the FSLN established the three resettlement camps where families could reunite with others from their village to work together for a better life and defend themselves more effectively. Together with the FSLN, they built solid concrete block houses that could not be burned, and they cleared land at the base of the hills south of Jalapa. Here they formed agricultural cooperatives and were able to obtain low-interest credit and other services from the government. As one of the monitors of the playgrounds project described this process and its results:

> Together they have built water systems, schools, and are now working on child care centers and health clinics. They feel very hopeful about their food production capacities and are growing crops such as beans, corn, melon, vegetables, and are also raising cows. The Santa Cruz cooperative, for example, was very pleased with the output of its potato crop in 1984 and is planning to clear more land for planting next year. They see this as their new home and the majority plan to continue living there even after there is no more fear of "contra" attacks. The people in these *asentamientos* consider them their new home and are working very hard in a relatively short period of time building and working the land. They feel more security and community support, espe-

cially the single mothers. These women have benefited tremendously from the new child care centers and children's dining halls being built to care for their children when they have to be working in the fields. They have much work ahead and there is a great shortage of supplies and means of transportation; yet they still have a strong hope and faith in their revolution and that their lives are improving.

PAIRING AND PEN PALS

Another dimension to these and other projects is more personal. It is hoped that any youth or school group that would raise money for the playgrounds or any other children's solidarity project would consider a pairing relationship with its Nicaraguan counterparts and correspond with them (contact the Institute for Peace and Justice for addresses and details). One of the spin-offs from the initial "solidarity parks" effort in Jalapa has been the opportunity for North American youth to correspond with Nicaraguan youth in Jalapa. Thirteen-year-old Isac Videa has invited North American youth to write him and his classmates in Jalapa (his address: de la casa cural, 2 cuadras al río, sector #4, Jalapa, Nicaragua).

In this and similar cases, *group* letters are preferable if an entire class or school wants to be involved—for example, a class letter instead of 30 individual letters, or better, individual letters mailed in one large envelope with the expectation of a single reply to the entire group. The letters should be written in Spanish. They should be personal—detailing the writer's interests as well as family and background information. The letters could describe solidarity activities the writer or class was doing on behalf of Nicaraguan youth—copies of letters to Congress or the President, of a letter to a newspaper editor or of an article on Nicaragua in a school or local newspaper or newsletter. These provide tremendous encouragement to Nicaraguans.

"PLAYGROUNDS, NOT BATTLEGROUNDS"

As more persons heard about the "solidarity parks" effort, it became clear that this effort should be expanded. Someone pointed out the irony implicated in the title of the expanded project—that as the Reagan administration was escalating the war against Nicaragua, building battlegrounds as it were, the children of the United States and Canada were building playgrounds. The Institute for Peace and Justice and the Inter-faith Committee for Latin America in St. Louis both agreed to take responsibility for the project and a number of national peace organizations agreed to become initial cosponsors—the Fellowship of Reconciliation, Pax Christi USA, and the Resource Center for Nonviolence in Santa Cruz, California.

> St Thomas Aquinas school
> Old Homestead road   Keswick Ont.
> Canada
>
> Friday May 18th 1984
>
> Dear Kids in Nicaragua
> When we first saw the slide show of you Miss Rowan our teacher and us Kids felt we needed to do something. We started hearing more and more about Nicaraguan people at war and refugee camps. So we decided to have a bake sale, for you Kids to have playgrounds, and we raised $65.00. We really hope that you can use it.
>
> yours truly
> the grade 5 class
> of St Thomas Aquinas school

While additional communities in Nicaragua that would take responsibility for the construction of playgrounds were being solicited, conscientization and fund-raising efforts began in North America on a very limited and decentralized basis. The "Amigos de los Niños" slide/tape presentation was completed and began to be shown in a number of schools and churches in the U.S.A. and Canada, as a way of communicating to children the reality of life for Nicaraguan children and how they as North Americans could be sisters and brothers to their Nicaraguan counterparts. Children are the main focus for this project and they have already come up with an amazing assortment of ways of generating funds and concern. They have sent money earned through special projects, and have made Lenten sacrifices. One girl asked everyone she invited to her birthday party to bring donations to the "playgrounds" project instead of a gift.

One family had friends send donations to the project in honor of their son's confirmation, and another gave pennies their children had earned during Epiphany for good deeds they had done. School classes have also participated in creative ways. One Canadian fifth-grade class constructed a model playground for their classroom as a visual reminder of what they were sacrificing and raising money for.

The most elaborate response to date has come from the first- and second-grade students at St. Leo's School in San Antonio, Texas. The teacher showed them the "Amigos de Los Niños" slide show. After discussing what they had learned, they drew pictures of playgrounds to send as a gift to the children of Nicaragua. Then they raised $49.42 by making little books of their stories and selling them. They sent the money along with the pictures they had drawn so that the children in Nicaragua could see them. They also took some photographs of their own playground to send to the children. Their teacher concluded enthusiastically: "My second-graders have amazed me at the depth of their understanding and commitment for peace. I showed them the slide show about the children of Nicaragua and they wanted to see it again. Now they talk about Nicaragua, El Salvador, and Guatemala with a simple knowledge."

COMMUNITY DEVELOPMENT IN LEÓN

The first Nicaraguan recipient of "playgrounds" money was Fundeci, a neighborhood organization in the city of León. Barbara Ginter, a Catholic sister, works with Fundeci and describes the history of the community as follows: "Fundeci was founded in 1973 by the Rev. Miguel d'Escoto.* Its purpose was the creation of a Christian community of a thousand low-income families. Both decent housing and integral personality development were envisaged. The families of this housing development would receive leadership training to participate as a community in programs of economic, cultural, social, educational, moral, religious, artistic, and athletic development.

"The work got going in May 1973. In collaboration with INPRHU (Institute of Human Promotion), university students were hired to conduct a survey among the marginal neighborhoods of León to locate families that needed housing and had the potential to be good community members. After the survey INPRHU held conscientization classes in different barrios of León for families chosen to participate in the program. In August 1974, a second-level course was given to these families, concentrating on home economics and community relationships.

"In September 1974, the first twenty-two families moved into the community. Construction was still going on to complete ninety-seven homes. Now that families had begun to move into the neighborhood, work focused on community formation. There were weekly meetings of all adults. They formulated their own *Manual del Vecino*. Biblical reflection, catechetical work, and pastoral work began. Different committees were formed, for sports, health, information and publicity, finance, community improvement, youth, women, and so forth. Each of these committees had its own board of directors, besides the overall board of directors for the whole community.

"It is important to note that while this community was being

---

* See Teófilo Cabestrero, *Ministers of God, Ministers of the People* (Fernando Cardenal, Ernesto Cardenal, and Miguel d'Escoto), Maryknoll, N.Y., Orbis; London, Zed Press, 1983, and the film Paraíso (see Resources) on this community.

built, the Somoza regime opposed it in several ways. Somoza demanded building permits for every 'block of cement that had to be laid,' and prices on materials rose sky-high.

"By June 1977, ninety-seven new homes had been constructed and occupied. The second phase of construction, to finish the thousand proposed homes, had to be delayed when the insurrection intensified. In November 1979, several months after the Revolution succeeded, Fundeci was turned over to the government and since then has been under the Ministry of Housing (MINVAH). Since that time, 545 new homes have been constructed. The people began to move into the homes by July of 1983. Today there are about 470 families occupying the new homes. The community has also started a preschool, which enrolls eighty children. The community has its own grocery store, and has renovated its community center, which was damaged during the war.

"Donations for playgrounds will be turned over to these families. This decision was made to further community development in the second phase. These 470 families had had no classes or courses in community development, and had moved in without knowing one another. Many came from a rural area and had never had to live closely with a group of others, let alone work closely with others to self-determine their own neighborhood. Community organization and leadership development is now the responsibility of the local CDS (Sandinista Defense Committee). These committees were set up in every neighborhood in Nicaragua after the 1979 triumph to further the goal of self-determination that the Revolution had promised the people.

"The 'Playgrounds, Not Battlegrounds' project is a gift at the right time for the people in the second phase. The board of directors of the neighborhood organization decided to build four playgrounds, which will benefit over two thousand children. The board of directors further proposed to the twenty community block clubs that compose the second phase that the money would be given, upon request, to groups that had a proven record in community participation.

"Before any donation was made, one block club in the second phase was already planning a fund-raiser for a children's park in its sector. It had had many clean-up days, showed good attendance at neighborhood meetings, was solidly involved in the neighborhood watch program, had many members volunteer to pick cotton, and so on. This group was held up as an example and was the first to receive some of the $1,500. It prepared a budget, continued raising some of its own funds, and designed its own playground. Its goal was to finish the playground by July 19, 1984, the fifth anniversary of the Revolution, and present it as an anniversary gift to the children.

"These were the plans for the first park, but one has to keep in mind that in Nicaragua materials are scarce, and the war complicates everything. We still have not been able to get the cement we needed to complete the project. As I write this report, there are outside my window three groups of infantry training for war. These kids look like they are 13 to 17 years old. The project 'Playgrounds, Not Battlegrounds' was very well thought out for Nicaragua. I just hope that the sites of the four proposed playgrounds do not themselves become battlegrounds.

"At the general meeting when the board of directors told the people about the playground project and the source of the funds, the people applauded all those in the U.S.A. and Canada who helped raise the money. Needless to say, they were filled with hope that at last things would be different for their children and they were all very grateful for the donation.

"I hope that the money will do more than build playgrounds for our kids. I hope that it will:

1. Promote better neighborhood participation and leadership development.

2. Help the people of the neighborhood realize the goals of the Revolution faster.

3. Give the people confidence in working together so they can continue to work together on other projects in the neighborhood.

4. Continue to restore their faith and trust in the American people who have so generously donated the money for these parks.

5. Be an example to other neighborhoods in Nicaragua, showing that if people work together as a community for the betterment of all, accomplishments can be made.

6. Cultivate the organizational skills that are needed and necessary in this neighborhood so that the people can continue *adelante* (forward, ahead) toward a New Nicaragua.''

As Barbara Ginter's report indicates, it was not until the fall of 1984 that the first playground was begun. Once completed, it will serve as a model for the other three. Additional funds are being sought to complete these playgrounds, and to implement the following projects.

OTHER PROJECTS

During the summer of 1984, several additional children's solidarity projects were proposed by Nicaraguans and efforts have begun to help finance them. The three described below offer, besides fund-raising possibilities, the possibility of a pairing relationship—between teenage youth groups in the first case and preschool or early childhood programs in the other two cases.

Youth Center in Jalapa

The FSLN youth coordinator for Jalapa sees a dire need for young persons there to have a facility to help them cope with the stresses of the war surrounding them, a place where they can relax with others, both teens and preteens. The building currently designated for the youth recreation center is the former Somoza National Guard headquarters in Jalapa, but it needs considerable work before it can be used as a recreation center. Plans have been drawn up for a game room, a dance hall, an auditorium for films and plays, and a snack bar. The first stage is the dance floor and auditorium. Costs for the first stage have been estimated at a little more than $2,000.

Early Childhood Program near Ocotal

Barrio Sandino is two kilometers outside Ocotal, a major city one hour's drive via dirt road southwest of Jalapa and a site of frequent "contra" attacks. This barrio has a children's dining hall (*comedor infantil*) that feeds 300 children a nourishing meal each day. Because many of the children live in single-parent homes with the mother working, they stay on the grounds after the meal. Workers at the *comedor* want to start a project to provide recreational activities for these children. They need approximately $2,000 for sports equipment, art and craft supplies, a record player, sheet music, and a number of musical instruments.

Partially completed playground at the Ocotal childcare center

*In the face of violence, the children will play;
in the face of loss, the children will sing;
in spite of the war, the children will make peace.*

Child Care Center in Ocotal

As described by one of the playground project monitors, "The child care center in Ocotal is one of the most beautiful I have ever seen, not because of elaborate equipment or materials (they have little), but because of how they love the children and the kind of nurturing environment they have created. There are lovely paintings of animals, birds, and plants on the walls—inside and out.

Gardens have been planted and a calm, child-centered atmosphere permeates the center. The children range in age from six months to six years. The workers have done an amazing job with little funding but much energy and hard work."

This child care center needs approximately $1,400 to complete the playground and to provide two water-filter systems for drinking water, sidewalks, toilets, and child-sized washbasins. Financial support for this project would also demonstrate moral support for hard work, dedication, and a mutual commitment to the nurturing of young children.

Flyers describing these projects are available from the Institute for Peace and Justice (see Resources). Checks (tax-deductible) for any of these projects should be made out to the Inter-Faith Committee on Latin America, and sent to the Institute.

Because these are all children's solidarity projects, adults are encouraged to involve (their) children as much as possible in relating to them. Fund raising should be done by the children whenever possible, and letter-writing and other details be their responsibility as well. The project organizers hope that adults will focus their Nicaraguan solidarity efforts on other critical projects described in this book but will also support children in their families, schools, churches, and communities in these children's projects—offering North American children the chance to live out the solidarity sentiment expressed at the beginning of this chapter in the statement accompanying the funds for the solidarity parks in Jalapa:

> . . . children who wish for their Nicaraguan brothers and sisters what children are supposed to have: laughter not tears, joy not grief, play not pain. . . . In the face of violence, the children will play; in the face of loss, the children will sing; in spite of the war, the children will make peace.

CHAPTER SIX

Nicaraguan Coffee: A Solidarity Buying Project

The story of Nicaraguan coffee is not just a factual account of the economic dependence of a Third World country on export cropping and on First World multinational coffee-processing corporations. Nor is it the story only of steps taken by the Nicaraguan government and popular organizations to lessen this dependency and to improve the life of the coffee workers and small producers. The story of Nicaraguan coffee is also the story of the people—of 15,000 volunteer harvesters in 1983, one of whom was 67-year-old Isabel Sirias; of Eugenio Amador, a leader in a new agricultural cooperative in Santa Cruz, near Jalapa; and of North Americans, hundreds of whom helped in the 1984 coffee harvest and thousands of whom are beginning to distribute Nicaraguan coffee and raise public awareness in the process, through efforts coordinated by Friends of the Third World in the U.S.A. and Bridgehead Trading in Canada.

There are a number of ways in which the specific solidarity project of buying Nicaraguan coffee can be helpful. First, it is a small but concrete way of benefiting Nicaraguan coffee producers and workers and supporting the efforts of the Nicaraguan government to develop an alternative agricultural system that benefits the poor. Secondly, distributing Nicaraguan coffee— through a local food co-op, a peace and justice group, or a church group—provides an opportunity to raise public awareness not only about Nicaraguan efforts to reorient the national economy to benefit the poor but also about the urgency of addressing U.S. government efforts to destroy the Nicaraguan Revolution. Thirdly, there are some related solidarity projects that flow from the coffee campaign.

ECONOMIC ANALYSIS AND OUR RESPONSE

Most of the following account is provided by Friends of the Third World (Fort Wayne, Indiana), as part of the public education component of its Nicaraguan coffee project. It is interspersed with background information on coffee production taken from *The World in Your Coffee Cup* (see Resources).

The Third World: Resource-rich, Dollar-poor

You may not know it, but a good portion of your early-morning routine comes courtesy of the Third World: the copper wiring in your radio alarm clock (Chile), the cotton in your sweatsuit (India), the rubber in your jogging shoes (Indonesia), the bananas in your breakfast cereal (Guatemala), the sugar in your coffee (Haiti), and the coffee (from Brazil, Colombia, etc.). These primary products come from the countries of Asia, Africa, and Latin America. These Third World countries, rich in resources, produce most of the "luxury foods" as well as much of the minerals and natural fibers that the industrialized First World consumes. With such an abundance of natural wealth, why is the Third World poor? The answer lies in its dependence upon First World countries for trade. The modern-day legacy of colonial relationships promotes underdevelopment of Third World countries in several ways.

First, many Third World countries have "single-crop" economies, dependent on the export of one particular commodity for foreign exchange. When the world market price of that commodity falls, that country's economy collapses. A drop of only 1¢ in the price of raw coffee, for instance, means a loss of some $65 million for the more than forty coffee-producing countries.

Secondly, it is usually in First World countries that primary goods are processed or made into manufactured goods. Giant multinational corporations control the technology and the capital that it takes to build new plants. When the new factories are built in the Third World by the multinationals, the profits flow back to the corporation, not to the workers in the plant. The raw materials that First World corporations buy each year from Third World countries are sold for $200 billion on the world market after processing. This provides a substantial profit for the corporations that control the terms of exchange.

In terms of coffee, three major corporations—General Foods (Maxwell House, Sanka, and other brands), Procter & Gamble

Diagram 2

Breakdown of Retail Coffee Costs

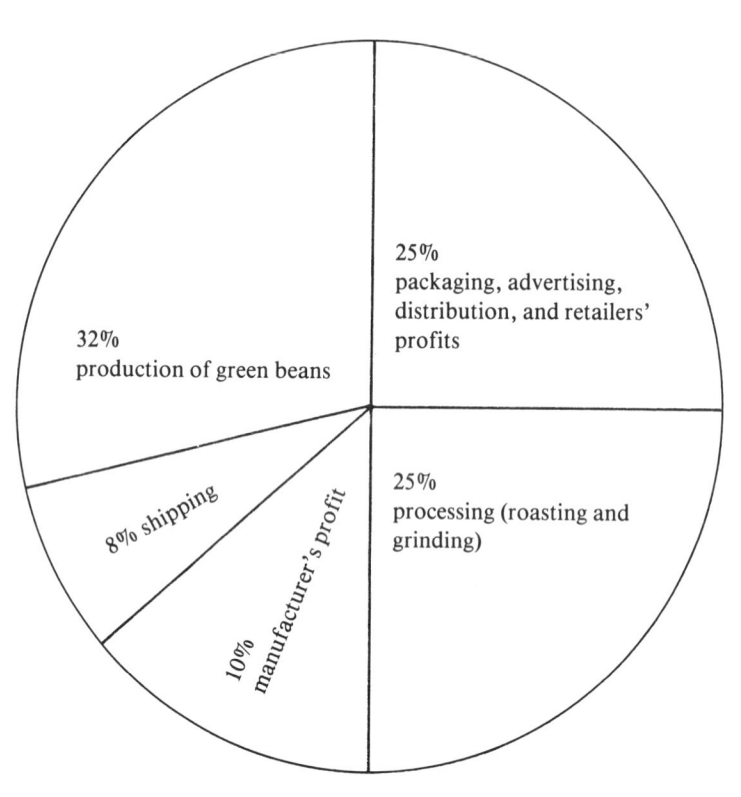

- 32% production of green beans
- 25% packaging, advertising, distribution, and retailers' profits
- 25% processing (roasting and grinding)
- 10% manufacturer's profit
- 8% shipping

(Folger's), and Nestle (Nescafe and others)—control the coffee-processing technology, dominate the markets in consumer countries, and thus reap the major profits. So large are these corporations that by the mid-1970s the total annual sales of General Foods and Nestle had exceeded the total *national* income of eleven of the fifteen largest coffee-producing countries in the world. No wonder that of these coffee-producing countries, only Brazil has been successful in developing a major coffee-processing industry. Thus, it is not surprising that, as Diagram 2 illustrates, less than one-third of the price we pay for our coffee goes toward the cost of the green (raw) coffee beans.

Thirdly, with the exception of crude oil, the relative value of most primary products has been falling in relation to the price of manufactured goods from the First World, which make up nearly 80 percent of the imports into Third World countries. The cost of these goods over the last several decades has risen dramatically with inflation and higher wages, whereas the cost of primary products has risen much more slowly. For example, the price of a jeep in 1955 was the equivalent of 124 sacks of coffee. Two decades later, a jeep costs 344 sacks of coffee. In 1977, one tractor cost 4.4 tons of coffee, but had jumped to 11.2 tons of coffee by 1981.*

Coffee as an Example of Inequities in World Trade

As a commodity in world trade, coffee is second only to petroleum in terms of the dollar amount traded each year. In the 1981–82 season, nearly 100 million bags of coffee were produced. That means 13 billion pounds of coffee picked, with 78 percent of it going to fill the cups of First World consumers.

More than 20 million persons earn their livelihood from coffee, most of them Third World farmers and agricultural workers. One-third of the world's coffee is grown on large estates of more than fifty acres, where substantial numbers of seasonal workers are employed. Half of the total production comes from medium-sized holdings, up to fifty acres, where seasonal labor is also required. Only one-sixth of the world's coffee is grown by small

---

* Joseph Collins, *What Difference Could a Revolution Make?* p. 11.

farmers with less than five acres of land. This means that the profits from coffee-growing are largely retained by landlords, rather than by the workers in the field in most Third World countries. Nicaragua and Tanzania are notable exceptions. The average coffee worker earns slightly more than $400 per year.

The U.S.A. imports more coffee than does any other country in the world, accounting for about 35 percent of all coffee exported each year. The average coffee drinker in the U.S.A. consumes 12.5 pounds of coffee each year. Coffee is the largest single food item imported into the U.S.A., amounting to more than $3.5 billion in annual sales. The corporations and sales distribution as of 1981 are shown in Table 2.

Table 2

U.S. Coffee Sales (1981)

Ground coffee	Instant coffee
#1 General Foods (Maxwell House) 40.4%/$880 million	#1 General Foods 46.5%/$650 million
#2 Procter & Gamble (Folger's) 23.3%/$510 million	#2 Nestle (Swiss-based) 26.0%/$360 million
#3 Hills Brothers 5.6%/$120 million	#3 Procter & Gamble 18.0%/$250 million
#4 Others 30.7%/$670 million	#4 Others 9.5%/$140 million

Source: *Alternative Trading News*, Jan.-Feb. 1984, p. 11.

The world coffee trade is regulated by the International Coffee Organization (ICO), which includes some forty-three exporting members and twenty-four importing members. In the early 1960s the International Coffee Agreement was drawn up in an effort to stabilize coffee prices through a system of yearly export quotas dictating how much coffee each producing country could sell. Al-

Coffee—Varieties, Growth Cycle, Processing

It takes 4,000 beans—the yearly harvest of about five trees—to produce one pound of coffee. Two major varieties are grown commercially. Arabica, a highland crop, is the best quality coffee. Washed arabicas, known as milds, are grown in Colombia, Central America, and East Africa. Unwashed arabicas, a slightly lower quality of mild, come mainly from Brazil. Robusta, the other important species, is grown in lowland areas of Africa. It has less flavor than arabica and is mainly blended with more expensive coffees for use in instant coffee.

Coffee requires a warm climate and flourishes only in the tropics. After the trees are several years old, fragrant white flowers bloom, and these soon develop into green berries. Six months later they ripen into red "cherries" containing two coffee beans. Lower grade coffees are prepared by the dry method: the red cherries are spread on the ground to dry in the sun for several weeks; the sun-dried cherries are then crushed in a hulling machine to remove the skin and pulp, leaving green beans. Better grades of coffee are produced by the wet method: red cherries are soaked in water for three days before hulling. Finally, green beans are graded and packed into 60-kilogram sacks for export.

When green coffee beans arrive in a consumer country, they normally pass through the hands of a dealer who sells them to a processor. The green beans are roasted in heated metal cylinders to bring out their flavor, and different varieties of coffee are usually blended together to improve the taste. Finally, the roasted beans have to be ground before they reach a coffee pot.

More and more beans are processed into instant coffee. It is manufactured by brewing freshly roasted and ground coffee in huge percolators. Using the spray-dried method, the brew is dispersed into small droplets. These are sprayed into a stream of hot air and the water is evaporated, leaving a powder of pure coffee. It takes about three pounds of roasted beans to produce one pound of instant coffee.

though the agreement was effective in putting a limit on price fluctuations, it also resulted in a decrease of close to 30 percent in coffee prices relative to industrial goods between 1963 and 1977.

The U.S.A., by virtue of its one-third share of world coffee imports, commands more votes in the ICO than does any other coffee consuming country. It has consistently vetoed any suggestion of indexing coffee prices to account for inflation and devaluation within the industrial world. As Penny Lernoux has written, "As long as there is no mechanism to compensate the developing countries for the loss of purchasing power, the rich nations can continue to buy cheap, sell dear, and maintain their standard of living at the expense of the developing world."

An Alternative Trading System

European groups have been working since 1968 to develop alternative trading organizations (ATOs) to bring producers and consumers together as trading partners. The goal of these groups is to import food commodities directly from Third World countries rather than through multinational corporations, to give producers a just price for their products, and to return part of the proceeds to producers to help finance worker-development projects. With the assistance of their European partner, Stichting Ideele of Holland, the Friends of the Third World decided in 1983 to initiate an alternative trading organization by importing and trading coffee from Nicaragua and Tanzania.

On July 19, 1979, the Nicaraguan people reclaimed ownership of its country following forty-three years of military rule under the Somoza dynasty. Under that dynasty 2 percent of the population owned 50 percent of the productive land; 70 percent of the rural population owned no land at all. The system guaranteed economic assistance to the few landed elites in control of the export market, whereas the majority of the rural population picked coffee and cotton for pennies a bag. Under Somoza most Nicaraguans had a hard time maintaining a hold on life. Health care was nonexistent. Malnutrition was the norm. Half of the adult population could not read or write. Those who spoke for change often paid for it with their lives.

Since 1979 the Nicaraguan people and the Sandinista government have been working together to build a food system that meets the needs of all the people. Children, mothers, and farmworkers—formerly the dispossessed in Nicaragua—are the subjects of change in Nicaragua today. Nicaraguan resources are now being used to boost production of staple foods, to build new clinics and schools in rural areas, and to continue the successful work of the literacy campaign.

The Nicaraguans are making efforts to diversify their export economy in order to achieve independence from the cotton and coffee markets. But this process takes time. As of 1984, coffee still accounted for 35 percent of Nicaraguan export income. And the dollars that Nicaragua earns for selling its coffee are essential in combating the economic and military campaigns being waged against it. Hospital beds, tractor parts, and medical supplies are all urgently needed and can often only be acquired with dollars earned from exports.

Because of its commitment to a "mixed economy," the Nicaraguan government has established policies that respect the private property rights of large coffee plantation owners and at the same time assist small farmers and hired farmhands. Between 1979 and 1983, sixty thousand small farmers joined together to form more than four thousand cooperatives. In most of these cooperatives individual families hold title to their own lands, while working together for government credit and services. The ATC (the rural workers union) and UNAG (the small farmers union) work to guarantee a living wage and adequate working conditions for previously disenfranchised workers. The incentives policy for agro-export production establishes a fixed price for coffee producers, which covers production costs as well as a guaranteed margin of profit. ENCAFE is the government coffee agency that coordinates coffee exports and manages all the coffee plantations formerly controlled by the Somoza family. Privately owned farms continue to be run by private owners who are taxed 60 percent of the net profits by the government and are required to provide each worker with certain standards of welfare, wages, and education.

Buying Nicaraguan Coffee
from Friends of the Third World

Friends of the Third World was founded in 1973 as a nonprofit organization concerned with the problems of hunger and poverty.

It supports the efforts of Third World peoples to become self-reliant and educates the public about these problems and efforts. In 1983, Friends of the Third World founded Cooperative Trading as an alternative trading organization to import Nicaraguan coffee (and other items). Between July 1983 and June 1984, it had imported twenty-seven tons of Nicaraguan coffee for sale in

Table 3

"When I buy a bag of Nicaraguan coffee, where does the money go?"

Per each 250-gram bag:

Purchase of raw coffee (from Nicaraguan stock stored in Holland)	$1.06
Foil bags (from Italy)	.04
Print and affix labels (by disabled adults in Amsterdam)	.01
Cardboard cartons	.01
Roasting	.13
Stichting Ideele overhead (nonprofit)	.06
Transportation and insurance to U.S.A.	.20
Customs entry into U.S.A.	.05
Dock pickup	.04
Freight forwarding, pallet breakdown, labeling	.05
Co-op Trading overhead	.10
Capital buildup for Co-op Trading	.04
Regional distribution points	.05
Trucking within U.S.A.	.29
Cost before retail markup	$2.13
Final sales price to customer after retail overhead markup	$2.50 to $3.00 per bag

the U.S.A.—through food co-ops, Central American solidarity groups, religious organizations, and many individuals, in forty-three states.

The coffee that Cooperative Trading offers is first shipped as green beans to Holland where it is roasted and packaged by Stichting Ideele, another nonprofit alternative trading group, and then shipped to the U.S.A. (Cooperative Trading is working to build up a volume of sales that will allow it to ship directly to small roasting plants in the U.S.A.). The Nicaraguan coffee is roasted from the top grade AA beans grown in the Matagalpa region of Nicaragua. Nicaraguan premium arabica beans are large, fancy roasters, boldly acid, full-bodied, and fragrant. Nicaraguan AA is similar to Guatemalan antigua yet distinctive in taste.

At present, Nicaraguan coffee is available as ground roasted coffee in vacuum-packed 250-gram packs (8.75 oz.), although Cooperative Trading also plans to offer roasted whole beans, restaurant packs, and water-processed decaffeinated coffee in the future. The minimum wholesale orders are based on the amount ordered. Individual packs are sold by mail order in any amount. Member groups of Cooperative Trading receive a 5 percent discount on all coffee purchases. Members also receive *Alternative Trading News*, a bimonthly newsletter, as well as the right to participate in project decisions through attendance at the annual conference. Annual membership dues for Cooperative Trading are $10. Cooperative Trading operates on a preorder basis. Orders are placed for the coffee every month and are shipped as soon as the cases arrive in either Philadelphia or Los Angeles by boat. Table 3 shows where our money goes when we buy a pack of Nicaraguan coffee through Friends of the Third World.

NICARAGUAN COFFEE—AND NICARAGUANS

In solidarity-buying projects, such as that of the Friends of the Third World, the personal dimension is at least as important as the economic dimension. Who are the persons involved in producing Nicaraguan coffee with whom we are standing in solidarity when we buy their produce? The February 14, 1983, issue of *Barricada International* printed the account that follows of the 1982–83 coffee harvest:

118 NICARAGUAN COFFEE

In December 1982, the alarm was sounded. The coffee crop had prematurely ripened in the departments of Jinotega and Matagalpa. The crop was in danger. The concern was justified since the two departments produce 60 percent of Nicaraguan coffee, which represents an income of U.S. $104 million for the country, equivalent to 20 percent of all exports for 1983. . . .

Not only was the coffee saved, but it ended up being a record harvest in Nicaragua—more than 70,000 tons of coffee. This achievement was primarily due to the massive mobilization of volunteer coffee harvesters, which at times included 15,000 people. . . .

When the call for volunteer harvesters was made, the country was also facing an increase in military incursions by Somocista units ["contras"] from Honduras; in the latter half of December these attacks resulted in 147 deaths, and 249 kidnapings, and left 72 injured. . . .

On December 18, it was estimated that 8,700 volunteer harvesters were needed. The actual number of volunteers, however, far exceeded that figure. Before the year had ended, some 8,300 harvesters—mostly members of the Sandinista Youth Association, state employees, and Sandinista Defense Committee members—were harvesting the crop in the northern mountains of Nicaragua. At the end of the harvest, in early February, the number had risen to 15,000, of which 11,000 were permanent volunteer harvesters. Thousands of others joined them on weekends.

The increase in counterrevolutionary activities in the region at that time was no coincidence. The goal was clearly to intimidate the harvesters and thus block the coffee harvest. As a result of the incursions by Somocista military units along the border, eight volunteer harvesters lost their lives, among them two children: Guadalupe Ruiz (age 13) and Pedro Joaquín Cruz (age 11). . . .

One of the volunteer harvesters was 67-year-old Isabel Sirias, who worked in the National Library in Managua. This is her story, as told to the poet Lizandro Chávez Alfaro and printed in *Barricada International* (Feb. 14, 1983):

It was the best experience in my 67 years. The most beautiful experience. I'd never been to a coffee plantation before, even though I've had to work very hard all my life. Because, to protect my children, I've always worked hard so they wouldn't have to suffer as I suffered. All of my children who wanted to study, studied; they studied and I supported them. I always tried to protect them. But really, with all that hard work, I've never been happier than I was in those coffee plantations. I asked God to give me strength, because of my age, you know; and I didn't have any problem climbing those hills. Oh sure, I got a little tired, but that was all.

It's unbearably cold in the north. The coffee pickers bathed at night, but they're young. I couldn't take a bath at night at my age because I have arthritis and varicose veins; so I knew it wouldn't do me any good. At 3:30 in the morning they started up a motor to grind corn for the workers. That's when I got up and bathed. When the water first fell on me, it was very cold, but after the bath I felt like new. By 5 A.M. we were in the kitchen for breakfast. Since the youngsters had to get out to the fields early, and there were so many people—60 of us and 60 *campesinos*—I helped serve the youngsters, washed dishes, and did whatever I could. At six in the morning, we went out to the fields to pick coffee.

It's really something to help your homeland, to raise production. And the most wonderful thing to me was when the person in charge asked if we wanted to be paid or to donate the money to the community. Almost everyone said yes, that they wanted to donate the money. Maybe three people said no and so it was agreed that if they didn't want to donate it, they would be paid. And that was beautiful, to have been able to make that contribution. It seems to me that maybe in the next year or so, a school can be built, or a clinic, and it would be wonderful for me to know that I contributed my grain of sand. That would make me very happy. . . .

The story of Eugenio Amador, a leader in a new agricultural community near Jalapa, provides a concrete sense of how things have changed for coffee workers since the Revolution. And it is persons such as Eugenio who ultimately benefit from our purchases of Nicaraguan coffee:

> Eugenio Amador has been a farmer in the Jalapa area since he was a youngster. After years of being a farm laborer, he and his family were able to buy a small farm on their own. Eugenio still depended on doing seasonal labor on a coffee plantation to supplement his income. The Namasli coffee plantation, located along the Nicaragua-Honduran border, paid starvation wages. Various attempts were made to unionize laborers there during the twenty years prior to 1979, resulting in violent repression by the National Guard who fiercely carried out the antilabor laws of the Somoza dictatorship.
>
> In the period of January to July 1979, the plantation owner, Adolfo Ramos, declared that he was opposed to the Somoza regime, but Ramos continued the economic exploitation of his workers. For four months prior to July 1979, Ramos refused to pay his workers, using the excuse that banks were too unstable to cash his checks.
>
> Following the success of the Revolution in July 1979, the workers learned that as workers they now had legal rights that the new revolutionary government would support. The workers then registered a legal claim for the back pay that Ramos owed to them. The new courts heard the workers' case and ruled in their favor. After Ramos paid the workers, he then fired them all so he could hire new workers at lower wages. Again, the new legal system protected the rights of the workers against injustice. Of course Ramos still had the right to own land and to produce coffee. If he paid his workers a fair wage, treated them with respect, and provided humane working conditions, he would be free to enjoy the profits of his enterprise.
>
> Apparently, Ramos felt that making a reasonable profit was not enough. Ramos took his machinery and other movable equipment to Ocotal, the departmental capital, and sold it for cash, which he took out of the country. He walked his cattle across the border to Honduras and sold the

herds there for U.S. dollars. By early 1982, he had abandoned the plantation and moved to Miami, Florida. In May 1982, the Nicaraguan government confiscated the abandoned farm. Now owned by the state and operated by the local community, the farm began to produce rice on the unused land, and yielded coffee in the December 1982-February 1983 harvest season. The people had great plans to make their living on this extensive, popular plantation. However, the counterrevolutionaries had more sinister plans.

Counterrevolutionary attacks began heavily on April 26, 1983. On May 2, 1983, the "contras" returned and burned the Namasli plantation. Four farmers were taken from their homes and killed. By June the entire area was under attack and Eugenio Amador and others who shared the Namasli land decided to evacuate to safer areas.

Many refugees who had fled the border towns joined in Jalapa and formed a farming cooperative. Present living conditions are crude, but work is rapidly progressing on a school, health center, and child care center. Women and men share responsibilities in marked contrast to pre-Revolutionary times. Eugenio said, "The people here fought in the insurrection and attained, after the triumph of July 19, 1979, the chance to change structures. The work of the Revolution is to transform people and social-economic relationships."

The strain to construct a new place and way of living is nearly impossible to bear in light of physical destruction caused by the "contras." People from outside the region are contributing. A Vermont group sent a starter herd of six dairy cows and calves in response to health needs of infants and nursing mothers at the cooperative where Eugenio lives and works [interview with Eugenio Amador by the WFP team in Jalapa, March 12, 1984, printed in *Nicaraguan Journal*, St. Louis Area Program of the American Friends Service Committee].

Because farming cooperatives like Eugenio's and the coffee cooperatives and plantations and other export crop operations are special targets for the "contras," whose tactics center on economic destruction and terrorization of the civilian population, solidarity efforts like that of the Vermont group and this Nicaraguan coffee project are especially appropriate.*

Finally, as a longer-term dimension of this Nicaraguan coffee project, the Friends of the Third World is asking individuals and groups distributing Nicaraguan coffee to set aside a percentage of their income from coffee sales to be donated back to Nicaragua for the development of a coffee processing plant, so that Nicaragua can benefit from the higher profits on the sale of processed coffee. The appropriateness of such action for U.S. citizens is made clear in the following description of a major "contra" attack on a coffee drying and processing plant in Ocotal on June 1, 1984:

> The "contra" force entered the plant at about 4:45 A.M. using gunfire and mortar attack from the ridge behind the electric company. A security guard there informed us that his work partner, Eusebio Cuadra, 55 years old, was attacked by gunfire as he ran toward the office building. He died almost immediately. He leaves a pregnant wife and eight children as well as various other dependents. The other security guard was injured but survived. The "contras" completely destroyed the office building, the machinery, two trucks, thirty-nine hundred pounds of coffee, and a part of the cement court used for drying coffee. The plant employs four persons full-time and thirty seasonal workers. Visual inspection of the area revealed hundreds of U.S. bullet shells and empty cardboard boxes marked NATO as well as "contra" propaganda pamphlets on how to commit acts of sabotage [WFP *Newsbrief*, June 18, 1984].

---

* Economic consequences of the war have been horrendous. Material damages primarily due to "contra" attacks on economic targets amounted to $128 million in 1983, equivalent to 30 percent of that year's export earnings. The mining of ports, according to *Envío* (May 1984), caused $9.1 million in damages. In 1983, 25 percent of the national budget was spent on defense, up from 18 percent in 1982. Shortages of basic goods due to these losses have been compounded by increased speculation and black market activities within Nicaragua. Medicaments especially seem to be in short supply, particularly in the countryside.

Besides an economic response to such destructive acts—raising money for Nicaraguan processing facilities or contributing to Nicaraguan emergency relief projects—we can publicize these acts and mobilize opposition to U.S. government support of them, in conjunction with the Witness for Peace effort in Nicaragua and the U.S.A.

CHAPTER SEVEN

Other Solidarity Projects

There is a considerable range of additional North American–Nicaraguan pairing projects, some long-term, some short-term. Several focus on direct economic or emergency assistance efforts to Nicaragua. Others embody the pairing concept of chapter 2. The story of La Granja, dealing with Nicaraguan prison reform, suggests its own version of pairing. Two other projects relate to the "solidarity buying" focus of chapter 6, on Nicaraguan coffee. Another lays open "work brigade" possibilities for North Americans. One—the Central American Peace Campaign—offers a legislative focus that can accompany any or all of the other solidarity projects.

LA GRANJA

Nicaraguan Prison Policies

The story of La Granja ("the farm") is a story of forgiveness and reconciliation that is reflected in other ways in Nicaragua, each a concrete example of the governmental commitment to a policy of national unity. One expression of this spirit is displayed on several billboards in the city of Managua: "If your enemy is hungry, give him something to eat; let goodness overcome evil."

The spirit of reconciliation is poignantly reflected in the life of Tomás Borge, the only living founder of the FSLN. Captured and tortured for months by the National Guard in the 1970s, he had his chance for revenge after the victory in July 1979. His torturers were taken prisoner, but instead of retaliation, Borge chose personally to forgive them. As recounted by Miguel d'Escoto, the Nicaraguan foreign minister, Borge said to them: "Remember when I told you I would take revenge when I was free? I now come for my revenge. For your hate and torture, I give you love; and for what you did, I give you freedom."

The new government immediately abolished the death penalty, set a 30-year maximum prison term, and by 1984 had released almost two-thirds of the seven thousand former National Guardsmen taken prisoner during the insurrection. The remaining prisoners are housed either at a former Somozan prison outside Managua (Tipitapa) or at unwalled prison farms.

At the prison in Tipitapa, prisoners are encouraged to work in the carpentry shop, the shoe-making shop, or one of the several other workshops. Resources are admittedly scarce. There are generally five prisoners to a cell, with a cell measuring twelve to fifteen square feet. Those who work are paid a wage, part of which is held in a savings account and part sent to their family. Workers are allowed visitors every Saturday. Those who choose not to work are allowed visitors every fifteen days. Many prisoners make crafts in their cells, with materials provided by their families who are also free to sell them. Prisoners are provided a Bible and allowed whatever other reading materials they want.

Once a week, a Roman Catholic sister, Mary Hartman, inspects the facilities and talks to prisoners to ensure that they are being treated as well as possible, given the serious limitation of resources. Prisoners and relatives of prisoners can and do file complaints that are Mary's responsibility to investigate as a member of the National Commission for the Protection and Promotion of Human Rights. Several examples reveal how serious the government is about human rights. Some prisoners in the police station in Grenada complained of verbal harassment and other mistreatment by four local policemen. Mary's office discovered the complaints were true. The government dismissed the four policemen and the entire department—because the others had known what was happening and did nothing to stop it.

A second example dates from November 1983. The national commission received a report from thirty-two Miskito Amerindians that they had been wrongly imprisoned. Mary and several lawyers from the national commission went to the "farm" that had been set up for captured Miskito counterrevolutionaries. After three days of investigation, they filed a report recommending that eighteen of the thirty-two prisoners be released. The next day, all eighteen were released. Mary's reflection on this incident is important, given the charges of totalitarianism, repression, and the violation of human rights in Nicaragua made by the U.S. government: "It's not that there are never any human rights violations in Nicaragua, but when there are, the government moves

Mary Hartman in front of her office

"It's not that there are never any human rights violations in Nicaragua, but when there are, the government moves quickly to correct them."

quickly to correct them." The next month, December 1983, the government declared an amnesty for all Miskitos who had left the country or joined the counterrevolution. Despite tremendous pressure from the "contras," more than two hundred immediately accepted the offer.

Justice and rehabilitation are the genuine aims of the prison system in Nicaragua. In July 1982, 130 college students volunteered to bring the now-famous Nicaraguan literacy program to the Tipitapa prison. For three nights a week, two hours a night, for five months, illiterate prisoners learned how to read and write and were exposed to the values and programs of the Nicaraguan Revolution.

Letting Dignity Work

This spirit of rehabilitation and reconciliation is reflected in a unique way in La Granja, the first of what are now seven unwalled prison farms. La Granja was begun in April 1982 as a means of transition, a step in reintegration into Nicaraguan society, for thirty-four former National Guardsmen in the final year or two of their prison sentences. These original thirty-four were chosen on the basis of their desire to participate and their record of cooperation at the Tipitapa prison.

La Granja covers 150 acres of farmland outside Managua. The prisoners farm about 100 acres of beans for themselves and their families, and care for a small dairy herd. La Granja now sells part of its harvest in an effort to become more economically self-sufficient. The prisoners have constructed their own simple kitchen, dining area, food pantry, and dormitory (in two sections so that there is privacy for conjugal visits). Perhaps the most unique aspect of the facility is that there are no guards, no weapons, only three "regulators" to oversee some of the farm operations. As such, no one is *forced* to stay. The prisoners clearly *want* the project to succeed so that it can be expanded in Nicaragua and serve as model for other penal systems.

The story of La Granja, then, becomes the story of its prisoners. In the original group of thirty-four, Arturo was the prisoner responsible for work and disciplinary matters. A lawyer, he had been a major in the National Guard. He spoke English and a little French. In explaining the operation of La Granja to a group of North Americans, mostly French Canadians, he chose to use English, with a French translation provided. This was a small but significant statement to us of his freedom to say what he wanted in the presence of the Spanish-speaking prison officials who accompanied our visit. He stated frankly that he considered himself a political prisoner, a prisoner of war, not a criminal, and that he was anxious to be free. After serving three years of his 11-year sentence, he would be released by the end of 1982. He was also insistent that there was no political reeducation in any direct sense, only the possibility of acquiring a skill and an opportunity for constructive work. "I believe in this project, but I'm not a Sandinista," he emphasized.

In private (officials insisted that we speak to the prisoners ourselves), Arturo elaborated on his statements, describing various ways in which prisoners were treated with respect. He told us of his own children and how he at first thought about taking advantage of the freedom to escape. "But no one," he added quickly, "has seriously considered escaping." Why? These men had clearly been incorporated into an experiment for which they felt personally responsible. They knew that any such efforts in the future depended on how well they performed. They wanted to make it work.

This determination was obvious in the person of Silvio, one of the two cooks at La Granja. He had been a supervisor in Somoza's Ministry of Labor but was clearly a *campesino* in character. As Arturo spoke to the group of visitors, Silvio made and handed out coffee and also some of the cookies brought the day before by his and other families (prisoners can have visitors every Sunday from 8 A.M. to 5 P.M.). Seeing the delight of our 11-year-old son Tom, Silvio returned several times with extra cookies. The sparkle in his eyes, the captivating warmth in his face, was powerful. He asked to address the group—the first time, we were later told, that he had spoken to a visiting group. "I want to open the door of your hearts, so that you won't forget me, won't forget this project, won't forget Nicaragua and what this revolution is trying to do." As if wanting to ensure that we would not forget, he gave several of us gifts—mesh storage bags he made. To Tom, he gave his own little bag for toothbrush and toothpaste. Mary

Hartman's comment about Silvio was profound: "When you treat others with dignity, they learn to respond with dignity." In a single sentence, that is the story of La Granja.

Silvio and Tom at La Granja

"I want to open the door of your hearts, so that you won't forget me, won't forget this project, won't forget Nicaragua and what this revolution is trying to do."

But the story of La Granja is also the story of its officials. One of them was Jorge Rostrán, director of rehabilitation for the Ministry of the Interior. He was a soft-spoken, gentle bachelor in his early 30s, a business administration student before the Revolution. He became active as a Sandinista supporter near the end of the Revolution and in October 1979 was chosen by the ministry for his present position. "I knew nothing about the job," he candidly admitted, "but they felt I was highly committed and a capable person. Qualified persons were extremely hard to find." He, too, was clearly proud of the La Granja experiment and was proud to say, "We want to make this the best prison system in the world."

Despite its early setbacks as a farm, the La Granja experiment eventually proved successful. The first crops were a complete failure, but little by little the prisoners learned more about the technicalities of farming. Experts came in and gave a 3-month course in agriculture. Now the prisoners are preparing the soil properly; they have an irrigation program and use some chemicals to control plant diseases. There are now fifty prisoners at La Granja. In addition to the weekly visits from their families, every six months the prisoners are permitted a week's vacation with their family.

Of the original group of thirty-four, all are now free. Arturo's wife and family returned from Miami and both he and his wife have "fine jobs" in Managua, according to Mary Hartman. Silvio is at his home on a farm in Chontales. Jorge Rostrán continues as director of rehabilitation, spending much of his time running in-service training sessions for persons working in the prison system. Mary describes the goal of this training as "to make persons in the security system better qualified to help create positive attitudes in prisoners, to better understand all types of conduct in prisoners, and to give better attention to the families of prisoners."

Because La Granja worked so well, there are now seven of these unwalled facilities, housing some seven hundred prisoners—criminals as well as former National Guardsmen. In the prison system as a whole and especially on the prison farms, the commitment to rehabilitation is clear and is always being expanded. Given the realization that individual rehabilitation is not possible apart from one's family, the system provides many opportunities for family visitation and is now experimenting with building small units where an individual can serve his prison sentence with his family living on the grounds. The objective is to change negative attitudes, to educate, to prepare prisoners technically for society, and to have them participate in activities (art, sports, culture) that help develop an integrated human personality. One specific example of this concern is that several times a year all the men on the seven farms get together for sports and cultural programs, "making for a healthy spirit of competition," in Mary Hartman's words. These concerns are reflected in the daily schedule on the farms—4 A.M. rising and work in the fields; noon meal and rest for three hours; lighter work until 5 P.M.; 6 P.M. dinner, followed by reading, artistic work, television.

How to Help

There are a number of ways in which North American groups can support La Granja and the other prison farms:
 1. Publicize these efforts, as a sign of what is really happening in Nicaragua.
 2. Raise money for the further expansion of La Granja and the other farms. Write to Mary Hartman, Apartado P-125, Managua, Nicaragua, for further information on how to help financially.
 3. Pair with one of the farms. Pairing possibilities are more numerous now that there are seven facilities. One creative pairing has begun. Alderson Hospitality House, opened in 1977 by Dick Dieter and Maggie Louden in Alderson, West Virginia, for family members of women imprisoned at the federal prison in Alderson, has linked with the original La Granja. Dick told the story of La Granja in one of his newsletters and is looking for other ways in which persons connected with his Hospitality House can relate to La Granja. Inquiries about pairing with any of these farms should be sent directly to Mary Hartman.

MEDICAL AID FOR NICARAGUA

Nicaragua faces an acute shortage of medicine. The October 1983 CIA attacks on the port of Corinto burned much of the nation's medical reserves. The spring 1984 CIA mining of ports made it difficult for Nicaragua to ship the farm products on which it depends for foreign exchange. Yet, as is evident from chapter 2 on Ciudad Sandino, Nicaragua continues forward with one of the most ambitious health care programs in the Western Hemisphere. Pure drinking water, vaccination of children, nutrition for pregnant women, breast feeding, oral rehydration therapy to stop diarrhea, malaria control, and free health care are resulting in a rapid drop in the disease and death rate in Nicaragua.

In response to the medical crisis due to the war, CONFER (Nicaraguan Conference of Religious) launched in November 1983 an international religious appeal for medical aid. The Maryknoll Sisters relayed the appeal to the U.S.A. and the Quixote Center in Maryland offered to coordinate the appeal and to collect and ship medicine and equipment. In Nicaragua it is the Association for the Development of the Peoples that receives and distributes the supplies through its extensive network of members of religious orders in Nicaragua. The association is an autonomous religious organization that gathers national and international support, provides technical assistance to local organizations, and builds up the community of faith. Besides medical supplies, the association seeks and distributes clothes for victims of war, food, tools, construction materials, seeds, and educational materials.

In the first six months of this effort, almost $1 million in medical aid was shipped to Nicaragua. In answer to the question of whether the medical aid gets there, Bill Callahan, S.J., of the Quixote Center writes:

> On April 26, 1984, a letter came from Sr. Margarita Navarro, who works in Nicaragua. While visiting the U.S.A., she collected medicines for the isolated town of Waslala in northern Nicaragua. We shipped the bags to her through the association. Later we heard from her:
>
> "*Muchísimas gracias!* The bags arrived. My part is already distributed in Waslala. Have you gotten news on the latest tragedies? April 3, Waslala was badly attacked by some 1,000 'contras.' . . . One of the Brazilian Sisters tells us that they cut people to pieces, alive and slowly, decapitated children, one an eleven-month baby; burned homes, the school, and the co-op; . . . there was no medicine to treat with. Sister came looking for help the day I was unpacking the medicine, so she carried it all back in sacks on the bus. Thanks to you all, some help got there. The aggres-

sion is every day getting worse. There are at least 8,000 'contras' within Nicaragua attacking small defenseless towns. Last week was *semana santa* (Holy Week)—and the sacrifice of 219 dead and 204 wounded."

In terms of how others can help, "Project Aspirin" is a relatively simple way to participate. Aspirin and Tylenol are badly needed. Local churches, schools, and community groups as well as individuals can take part. Label packages "Quixote Center—Project Aspirin," and send to the second of the three addresses listed in Table 4.

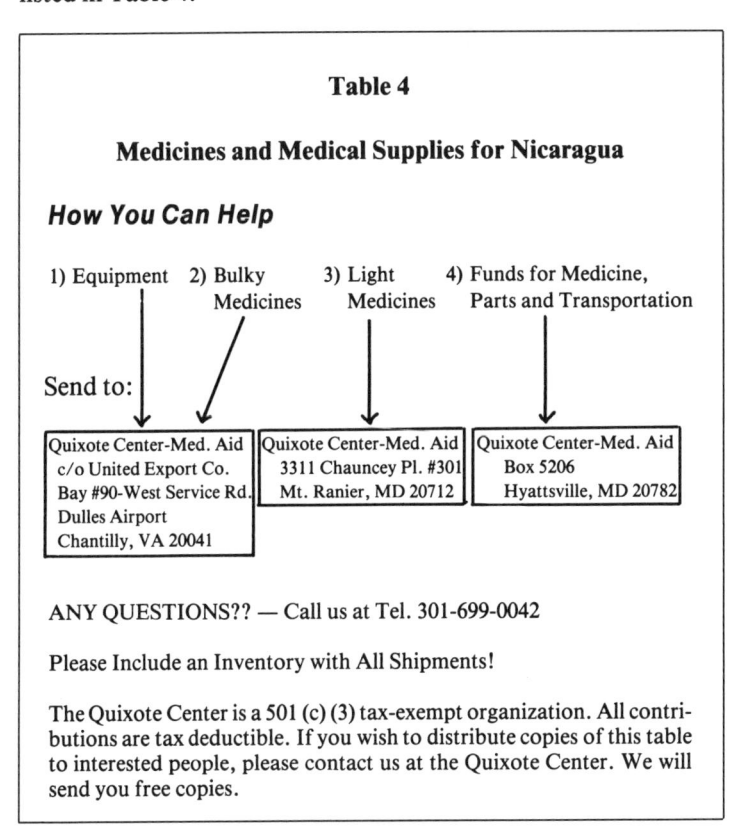

Table 4

Medicines and Medical Supplies for Nicaragua

How You Can Help

1) Equipment   2) Bulky Medicines   3) Light Medicines   4) Funds for Medicine, Parts and Transportation

Send to:

Quixote Center-Med. Aid c/o United Export Co. Bay #90-West Service Rd. Dulles Airport Chantilly, VA 20041	Quixote Center-Med. Aid 3311 Chauncey Pl. #301 Mt. Ranier, MD 20712	Quixote Center-Med. Aid Box 5206 Hyattsville, MD 20782

ANY QUESTIONS?? — Call us at Tel. 301-699-0042

Please Include an Inventory with All Shipments!

The Quixote Center is a 501 (c) (3) tax-exempt organization. All contributions are tax deductible. If you wish to distribute copies of this table to interested people, please contact us at the Quixote Center. We will send you free copies.

Medical and dental supplies needed in Nicaragua are listed in Table 5 (drawn up by the Quixote Center).

Table 5

Medical and Dental Supplies Needed in Nicaragua

MEDICAL SUPPLIES

Sutures
EKG machines
Syringes—3, 4, 10 cc
Syringe needles
Scissors
Anteriogram syringes & needles
Instruments for minor surgery—clamps, forceps, scalpels, suture holders
Stethescopes
Opthalmoscopes
Otoscopes
Batteries for opthalmoscopes
Clinic scales/bathroom scales
Infant scales—prefer spring w. hook
Thermometers—rectal and oral
Gauze—any size
Adhesive tape—any size
Peroxide
Disposable gloves—sterile/nonsterile
Intravenous catheters, solutions, tubes
Incubators
Crash carts
X-ray film, developer, fixadent
Ice bags
Blood tubes
Specimen containers
Fever strips
File boxes
Urine dip sticks
Measuring tapes
Fetescopes
Doptone
Hemoglobinometer
Hemolyses sticks for hemoglobinometers
Wheelchairs—adult & child
Band aids
Betadine solution
Alcohol
Catheters
Endotrachial tubes
Splint & cast supplies
Obstetrical forceps
Epidural kits
Thoracentesis kits
Lumbar puncture kits
Masks
Speculums
Laryngoscopes
Nasogastric tubes
Suction tubes
Foley catheters
Blood pressure cuffs
Catgut

Table 5

Medical and Dental Supplies Needed in Nicaragua

MEDICINES

Antihypertensives	Antibiotics
Vitamins—prenatal, child/adult	Analgesics
	Antiinflammatories
Skin ointment	Gastrointestinals
Vitamin E oil	Antiarrhythmics
Eyewash	Hydrocortisone cremes
Antiemetics	Flourinated steroid cremes
Malarials	
Antispasmodics	Medication for worms
Expectorants	Ferrous sulfate
Antifungal cremes	Anesthetics—local/general
Antidiarrheals	
Mecurochrome solution	Bronchodilators
Diuretics	Antihistamines
Anticonvulscants	Antitoxins
Hormones	TB & Mantoux
Anticoagulants	Antipararasitics
Immunizations	Vaginal cremes/suppositories

DENTAL SUPPLIES

Instruments	Masks
Substance for fillings	Tooth-cleaning materials
Gloves	Any items of use in a local dental clinic

Besides medical supplies, the Quixote Center is also collecting and shipping school supplies to Nicaragua. Smaller items, such as pens, pencils, crayons, and notebooks, can be sent to the third address in Table 4; larger boxes of supplies should be sent to the first address in Table 4.

AFSC NICARAGUA APPEAL

The American Friends Service Committee has a very impressive record in its development and aid projects. It focuses on school supplies (paper, pencils, rulers, maps, paints, crayons, etc.), and medical supplies. The first shipment, worth $185,000, was sent in April 1984, with others to follow. Checks should be made out to "Central American Assistance Fund." Packages should have a note attached describing the contents.

Other medical aid projects have been organized by the Nicaraguan Medical and Material Aid Campaign (19 West 21st St., New York, NY 10010).

TOOLS FOR PEACE

Oxfam America is an international nonprofit development agency, one of whose many excellent projects in Central America was a spring 1984 campaign to send a shipment of tools and spare parts to Nicaraguan farmers so that they could grow their own food. The campaign may well be extended. Contact Oxfam America for further information.

HUMANITARIAN AID FOR NICARAGUAN DEMOCRACY (HAND)

HAND is the humanitarian aid arm of the National Network of Solidarity with the Nicaraguan People (see Resources). It has been aiding Nicaragua for several years. In the fall of 1983, NNSNP/HAND launched a "U.S. Citizens Reparations Campaign" to begin compensating the Nicaraguan people for damages caused by U.S. government intervention. The campaign has involved two components: sending volunteer work brigades to Nicaragua (see below) and promotion of the HAND fund to collect humanitarian aid for Nicaragua in three priority areas—health care, emergency aid for displaced persons, and a project to bring electricity to the Miskito settlement of Tasba Pri.

In accordance with the needs of the Nicaraguans and with the approval of the Coordinating Committee, we will include educational assistance funds and agricultural projects in the HAND campaign. Both of these sectors have been key areas of progress and increased popular participation in the new Nicaragua through the National Literacy Crusade, the adult basic education program and agrarian reform. Precisely because of that progress and participation, they have both been special targets of the counterrevolution and have suffered tremendous human and material loss. In education alone, 150 teachers have been killed, 15 schools destroyed and another 27 prevented from being built. Also, 647 adult basic education collectives (those that continue the literacy crusade, teaching grades 1-6 to adults) and 138 primary schools have had to be abandoned. Both of these sectors rely in part on products that are not presently produced in quantity in Nicaragua such as pencils, paper, livestock vaccines, tractor parts, etc.

WORK BRIGADES FOR NICARAGUA

More than six hundred North Americans participated in the 1983-84 coffee and cotton harvests as members of various volunteer work brigades. For further information on future possibilities, contact Bob Sanders, Philadelphia Coffee Brigade, 330 W. Logan, Philadelphia, PA 19144; 215-843-8320; or Volunteer Harvest Brigades Project, Nicaragua Exchange, 239 Centre St., New York, NY 10013; 212-219-8620. The NNSNP is also organizing other "technical brigades" in engineering, energy production, and agriculture, and a variety of "project brigades" in answer to requests for assistance on specific projects such as painting a school or helping in the construction of a community center. For information on health care brigades, contact the Central America Health Rights Network/East (Dick Garfield, 212-694-3944) or the Committee for Health Rights in Central America (Jan Diamond, 1827 Haight St., Box 5, San Francisco, CA 94117; 415-821-6471).

PEOPLE-PANTS AND SPARE PARTS

Another way to support Nicaraguan workers and the Nicaraguan economy is by the purchase of cotton pants ("people-pants," as they are called) through the Union of Third World Shoppes sponsored by the Friends of the Third World. As their newsletter describes the project:

We are now able to sell pants produced by Nicaraguans at up to 6,000 pairs per month. We are able to sell them for about $18 retail and $12 per pair wholesale to groups who wish to help sell them. These are finely made for either men or women and come in even sizes—26, 28, 30, 32, etc.

As with many areas of industry in Nicaragua, there is a need for repairs to the sewing machines that are used to produce these pants. We have found the repair parts they requested. They are available at a cost of $913.50, with shipping costs to be $54.33, for a total of $967.83. We need to raise these funds within the next three weeks to get this project going.

Friends of the Third World was successful in raising this money, and the project has begun. Additional donations are needed for additional spare parts.

PUEBLO-TO-PEOPLE

Pueblo-to-People describes itself as a nonprofit, nonsectarian foundation formed by individuals who are concerned about the situation of the poor majority of Central Americans. "We believe the solutions to the problems engulfing the area must come from those affected, and not from the outside. We feel that the main problem is the concentration of power and resources in too few hands. Therefore we are supporting democratic, grassroots organizations of rural and urban poor who are collectively working for meaningful change in order to reduce the difference between the 'haves' and the 'have-nots.' As foreigners with experience in Central America, we feel that our most logical role is to open up channels of informational and economic interchange . . . in a way that is beneficial rather than exploitive."

Pueblo-to-People makes available a variety of handicrafts—from mahogany sling rocking chairs ($30) and mahogany cassette racks ($9 and $14) to cashews ($7 per pound), hammocks ($39), potholders ($4), and assorted other wood and hand-woven products—from El Salvador, Guatemala, Honduras, and Nicaragua. From Nicaragua, Pueblo-to-People has available coffee

and wooden plates, with other items to be added later.
The wooden plates come through a barter agreement with a cooperative of artisans in Monimbó. The co-op, Cooperativa Mariano Yaméndez, agreed to an arrangement whereby Pueblo-to-People would supply band saw blades in exchange for wooden plates. The arrangement provides the artisans with saw blades at half the price they were previously paying. The Cooperativa Mariano Yaméndez is named after a martyr of Monimbó who was killed by the National Guard in September 1978 when he was 25 years old. It was started by the Ministry of Culture in April 1980 with sixteen workshops.

It is not a coperative in the sense that the workers own and control the enterprises but is rather a cooperative of workshops. Each workshop is privately owned. Most of them are small, having only one or two workers. The largest has fifteen workers. There is definitely a political consciousness in the co-op, stressing responsibility to workers and vice versa. The main purposes of the organization are to purchase supplies together—most of them imported—and to divide production among the shops according to capacity and skill.

MADRE

MADRE is a network of small groups of women who know each other through their jobs, their children's schools or day care centers, through community or political work, churches and synagogues, or meetings in parks and playgrounds. Letter-writing and twinning enable MADRE groups in the United States and Central America to connect the realities of each other's lives and hopes. Small groups work together on fund-raising vigils, regional and national events, petition campaigns, friendship tours, and media work.

Letter-writing: In letters, mothers in the United States and Nicaragua can share thoughts and experiences, becoming more familiar with each other's worlds.

MADRE photographs: Every U.S. member receives an identification card with a photograph of a Nicaraguan mother. Every North American woman wearing the ID card reminds others that there is a woman in Nicaragua with the same hopes and concerns for her loved ones.

Twinning: Twinning is the pairing of local institutions such as day care centers, schools, or clinics with similar institutions in Nicaragua for joint educational work or fund-raising. Twinning provides a telling insight into daily life in Nicaraguan communities, and highlights concrete needs at home. A fund-raising drive to support a children's clinic in your town can also supply needed medical care for the children of a town in Nicaragua. MADRE can supply each twinning group with an appropriate contact group in Nicaragua, and inform it of resources and materials for organizing local projects. Individual members and friends of MADRE groups are often relied on to initiate or do the leg work for local twinning activities.

Friendship tours: Exchange tours between North American and Nicaraguan mothers help dispel myths and fallacies and strengthen human bonds. Tours are coordinated by the MADRE office and hosted by local members in both countries.

Fund raising for material aid: The economic damage resulting from U.S.-sponsored attacks on Nicaragua has been crippling. The Managua airport, several major ports, and key commercial roads have been bombed. MADRE has called on women and men throughout the U.S.A. to participate in emergency drives to send vitally needed supplies to Nicaragua. Through donations of goods or money, MADRE can help Nicaraguan mothers sustain the lives of their families. Slide shows, parties, bake sales, teach-ins, concerts, film showings, rummage sales, dinners, street fairs, art exhibitions, or poetry readings can help educate others about what is going on in Central America and also involve them directly by raising funds or collecting lifesaving, emergency supplies.

Town meetings: At regular or specially called town meetings, connections can be made between local concerns (the need for social services, health care, schools, jobs, safety, and a desire for peace) and similar problems in Nicaraguan communities, and between the effect of U.S. policy at home and in Central America. Information on life in Nicaragua today can be obtained through the MADRE office, 853 Broadway, Room 905, New York, NY 10003; 212-777-6470.

FR. BERNIE SURVIL

After working elsewhere in Nicaragua and El Salvador for many years, U.S. Catholic priest Bernie Survil arrived, in September 1983, in the mountain town of Esquipulas, almost on the continental divide, in the heart of Nicaragua. This region of Matagalpa has some 250,000 inhabitants, mostly in villages. Bernie's parish serves a number of these villages. In writing about one of them, Portón, he states: "... it has had no school classes since the counterrevolutionaries came sweeping through in March 1983. Most foreign doctors such as the West German ones and the Cuban teachers were threatened by the 'contras' and thus forced to abandon their volunteer service in the mountain areas such as ours. Part of the dividends of the U.S. covert military aid are hundreds of kids in my parish alone who are losing a year's schooling."

Contrasting the attitudes of the small farmers in his parish with those of the workers on the privately owned and state owned *haciendas* where "an environment of dependency" prevails, he further writes: "What a contrast is offered by the small farmers of our parish who provide most of the candidates for lay pastorates, build their own chapels, and even travel on foot to help other villages with religious instruction."

It is particularly for these dedicated lay religious educators that Bernie is seeking help. As he describes the need and the response:

> Since returning to Nicaragua and being assigned to this parish, a lot of wonderful people have sent packages of instructional materials for our religious education program, items like pencils, pens, crayons, water colors, desk supplies, coloring books, and also small recreational items like picture puzzles, checkers, chess pieces, jump ropes, guitar strings, recorders, used Christmas cards, and, as always, used eye glasses. These basic supplies are most appreciated and can continue to be sent—through the Latin American Project, Thomas Merton Center, 1111 E. Carson St., Pittsburgh, PA 15203; 412-381-1400; packages and mail can get to me c/o Apartado 2847, Managua, Nicaragua.

A U.S. peace center newsletter has noted that Bernie is also asking for packets of cabbage seeds, a very inexpensive item to mail.

Bernie writes regularly to those who write to him, and he is always looking for ways in which to pair his parishioners with counterparts in North America. His parish address is: Bernard Survil, Casa Cural, Esquipulas, Nicaragua.

CENTRAL AMERICA PEACE CAMPAIGN: "TALKS, NOT TROOPS"

This campaign was begun in January 1984 by a group of organizations working against U.S. military intervention in Central America: the American Friends Service Committee, the Caribbean Basin Information Project, the Coalition for a New Foreign and Military Policy, the Commission on US/Central America Relations, SANE, Committee in Solidarity with the People of El Salvador, the Institute for Policy Studies, the Inter-Religious Task Force on El Salvador and Central America, the National Labor Committee in Support of Human Rights and Democracy in El Salvador, the National Network in Solidarity with the People of Nicaragua, the Network in Solidarity with the People of Guatemala, the Religious Task Force on Central America, and the Washington Office on Latin America.

The primary goal of the campaign is to move beyond merely defensive activities in response to Reagan administration initiatives and to develop a longer-term plan for developing widespread public support for an alternative policy in Central America, which will substitute diplomacy, negotiations, and appropriate economic assistance for the current policy of military intervention. The foundation of the campaign is the program/platform statement *Changing Course: Blueprint for Peace in Central America and the Caribbean* (see "The Blueprint in Brief," p. 23, above), a document endorsed by many leaders of religious, labor, and peace organizations, elected officials, and scholars. "Talks, Not Troops" was the slogan chosen to capture the twofold idea of promoting a positive alternative (negotiations) and opposing U.S. military intervention in the region.

The initial focus of the campaign was the 1984 elections. Convention delegate education and public initiatives during the Democratic convention were followed during the fall by voter education (house meetings, town meetings, petition canvassing), local organizing efforts including local government resolutions and referendums, letters to editors and op-ed pieces, public service announcements, and the like.

As a longer-term legislative vehicle, in addition to ongoing work in Congress around specific military aid bills, the "Talks, Not Troops" program has been translated into a package of bills that embody Central America Peace Campaign principles and will be introduced in Congress in January 1985 as the "Central America Peace Initiative for 1985." The point here was not to put forth something that would immediately be acted on by Congress, but to use the "peace package" as a long-term tool for organizing broad support for a positive alternative to the Reagan policy. This legislative package tries to have enough substance to it to make it worth fighting for and be realistic enough that progressive Democrats and some Republicans can be persuaded to support it as cosponsors.

CHAPTER EIGHT

The Inner Core of Solidarity

The reflection on Christian unity presented in chapter 3 by the ecumenical youth leaders focuses on the interior dimensions and sources of unity and solidarity. We are called to be "one body." There is only one God, a loving Creator/Parent whose Spirit is the source of our unity, our being brothers and sisters with every human person. How to realize this call in ourselves and promote it for others—how to allow the Spirit to create this oneness or solidarity in and through us—is our ultimate vocation. There are many elements involved in this process, including side-by-side service with those who are suffering, simplicity of lifestyle, prayer, and fasting. The more these elements become an integral part of our lives, the more likely we are to take up, persevere in and be willing to take greater risks in our solidarity actions and projects.

SIDE-BY-SIDE SERVICE

Two aspects of oneness or solidarity can be experienced in direct service with persons who are suffering. First, their lives and stories get inside us, haunt us, as it were, call us to work for change because of our relationship with them. This is part of the reason for pairing and for the stories in this book—to allow the lives of those who are victims of injustice, who are struggling for change, to touch our hearts and thus move us to more generous, courageous, and persistent action.

Secondly, direct service work develops our capacity to love. Whether it is involvement in a hospitality house, a soup kitchen or food pantry, prison or hospital visitation, or in the less formal ways of being available to others through our home, our phone, our office, we are learning how to love, and to love others perhaps very different from ourselves and generally not ones whom society considers "beautiful." They are persons who can stretch our hearts to embrace a wider segment of God's family (and often they are the ones who show us what love and courage are all about).

For these and other reasons, Gandhi included as an essential dimension of his "formation" program for himself and his fellow "satyagrahis" (nonviolent resisters) what he called "constructive work" in the villages. Satyagrahis were to work side-by-side with the poor, with those *with* whom as well as *for* whom they were working for change. This connection between solidarity and service is at the heart of the poetic reflections of Javier Torres and Orlando Pérez, leaders in the MJCI (see chap. 3).

SIMPLIFYING OUR LIFESTYLE

Solidarity with the whole human family and with God, as well as action on behalf of justice, are very difficult if not impossible if we live immersed in material comforts. Reducing the number of material goods we depend on, as well as our attachment to them, can help us become more single-minded in living our faith and responding to our call. No person can serve two masters. We need to root out the obstacles or attachments in our lives that keep us from risking and from loving more fully. Being too comfortable can also dull our sense of urgency and passion for justice. We are called to "hunger and thirst" for justice, not dabble at it in our spare time. Further, learning to live on less and less can help us identify more fully with the majority of the human family who have little in the way of material goods. Finally, the self-discipline involved in simplifying our lives can help us become a more fit instrument of solidarity.

Committing ourselves to justice demands a willingness to take risks and to persevere for a lifetime. Spiritual, mental, and physical stamina is essential. For those who are able, physical condi-

Oración

Señor mi Dios
hoy he decidido amarte
sin golpearme el pecho
sin el sencillo de mi bolsillo
sin orarte arrodillado, allá al frente, en el centro
sin visitas a diario al templo
sin cantos hipócritas
sin palabras vanales
y hasta sin gritarte Aleluya!

Señor Dios mío
con los niños de los basureros de los mercados
con los niños voceadores, vende frutas, cuida carros
con los lustradores
con los campesinos desposeídos de sus tierras
con los obreros que aumentan el capital de otros
con las madres que venden su carne y compran el pan a sus hijos
con los ancianos olvidados en las calles
con los retardados mentales asoleados y hediodos
con los picaditos alcohólicos anónimos de los barrios
con todos los minusválidos desamparados
y a través de ellos he decidido amarte.

Señor, he decidido amarte
en darles a ellos lo que tengo
porque Vos me lo has dado
no para mí
sino para ellos.

ORLANDO PÉREZ V.

Prayer

Lord, my God
today I have decided to love you
without beating my chest
without change in my pocket
without praying on my knees, down front, in the center
without daily visits to the church
without hypocritical hymns
without banal words
even without crying out Alleluia!

Lord, my God
together with the children of the market trash collectors
with the shouting children, the fruit vendors, car watchers
with the shoe shiners
with the farmers dispossessed of their lands
with workers who increase the capital of others
with mothers who sell their flesh to buy bread for their
    children
with the old people left forgotten on the streets
with the mentally retarded
with the anonymous alcoholics of the neighborhoods
with all the helpless handicapped people
and through them I have decided to love you.

Lord, I have decided to love you
by giving to them that which I have
because what you have given me
is not for myself
but for them.

ORLANDO PÉREZ V.

El Hambre de Otros

Si el hambre de otros no es mía,
Si la angustia del vecino en todas sus formas
   no me pertenece,
si la desnudez de mi hermano
   no me atormenta,

entonces yo no tengo ninguna razón
   de ir a la iglesia y vivir.

La vida es: amar al prójimo
   como a uno mismo;
es el mandamiento de Dios.
Amores son hechos y no buenas razones.
Por eso estoy integrado al trabajo,
   por las necesidades
   de mis hermanos.

The Hunger of Others

If the hunger of others is not my own,
If the anguish of my neighbor in all
   its forms touches me not,
If the nakedness of my brother
   does not torment me,

then I have no reason
   to go to church and to live.

Life is this: to love one's neighbor
   as oneself;
this is the commandment of God.
Love means deeds, not good wishes.
For this reason I commit myself to
   working for the necessities
   of my brothers.

JAVIER TORRES

tioning can help prepare us for the challenge of working for justice and peace. We cannot, in the words of Martin Luther King, Jr., "stand up for justice," while we are lying down and enjoying a life that does not involve some kind of physical and mental discipline.

PRAYER

For more than one reason, prayer is important for sustaining our solidarity actions and deepening an inner sense of solidarity. First, prayer is crucial in our search for clarity or vision. Reflecting on the word of God and on the events of our day and the world, we seek to understand the personal and cultural obstacles to hearing and acting on God's Word and we seek to understand God's way and view of our world. In particular, prayerful reflection on the Hebrew prophets can help us discover our own prophetic mission, realize God's sustaining love in the midst of suffering, and become more convinced of God's covenant or promise of shalom—the promise that energizes our efforts and sustains our hope. Prayer provides the opportunity for a unity or empathy with the whole human family—the internal bond that inspires and informs our external actions for justice. The more we lift up the lives and needs of others in prayer, the more we experience an inner sense of solidarity with them.

Finally, prayer provides an opportunity for becoming more aware of the presence of God and God's Spirit in our lives and in the world. Reflective moments provide an opportunity for us to discover that we are loved, gifted, and sent forth—essential if we are to act for justice perseveringly.

Meditating on the paschal mystery helps us discover the appropriateness of our struggle for and celebration of justice, of our own death and resurrection, and of the death and resurrection of others. Henri Nouwen experienced this deeply through his encounter with the Nicaraguan people and articulates it in a beautiful reflection entitled "Christ of the Americas":

> Here we touch the spiritual dimensions of all social concern. The hunger of the poor, the torture of prisoners, the threat of war in many countries, and the immense human suffering

we hear about from all directions can only call us to a deeply human response if we are willing to see in the brokenness of our fellow human beings the brokenness of God, because God's brokenness does not repulse. It attracts by revealing the loving face of the One who came to carry our burdens and to set us free. Seeing the agony of the people then becomes the way of coming to know the love of God, a love that reconciles, heals, and unites. . . .

After this reflection on the death of Christ, Nouwen focuses on the resurrection:

Christ is risen means that Christians are a people of reconciliation, not of division; people who heal, not hurt; people of forgiveness, not of revenge; people of love, not of hate; in short, people of life, not of death.

When I heard the words of forgiveness spoken by the five Nicaraguan women in Jalapa, my paralysis about how to speak about Central America was gone. I knew that these women had empowered me to return to my people and to call them in the name of the Risen Christ to their task of peacemaking. I could do this now, not because I feel guiltridden and want to clear my conscience but because I had heard the words of God's reconciling forgiveness that are words for all the people of North America. . . .

Now the time has come to accept the forgiveness offered to us and realize that we belong to one body. Now the time has come to reach out to our suffering sisters and brothers and to offer food, shelter, and health care. Now the time has come to heal the wounds of centuries and make visible to the whole world that Christ is risen indeed. Let us be peacemakers as we are called to be and thus come to realize that we and all the people of South and Central America belong to the household of God and can indeed be called God's children.

It seems essential that we start realizing that our first task toward the South and Central American people is not to do something for them, not to help them with their problems or to assist them in their needs. All of that is very important, but all forms of help become forms of violence when giving does not presuppose receiving. Our first task is to receive from the suffering people the fruits of their suffering. Only then can we truly give. We need the people of South and Central America as much as they need us. We need one another as much as members of the same body need one other. In the midst of the present international crisis, we are becoming aware in a new way that not just our physical and emotional well-being but also our spiritual destiny—our salvation—cannot be realized without the people of South and Central America. We need them for our salvation. They offer us forgiveness, gratitude, joy, and a profound understanding of life as mature fruits of their struggle for freedom and human dignity. They offer us these fruits for our conversion, so that we too may be saved. By their suffering they have indeed been ordained to be our evangelizers. It may be hard for us to recognize this divine irony by which the oppressed become the healers of the oppressor, but it is this recognition that might be the beginning of our conversion. While it is true that the Resurrection of Christ has become manifest in a totally unexpected and new way among our suffering and dying fellow Christians in South and Central America, we will only be able to become real witnesses of the Resurrection when we allow these Christians to become our spiritual guides. Then and only then are we free to help them, not out of obligation, guilt or fear, but out of gratitude for the gifts we already have received. Thus we can become together again one people, the people that manifest the risen Christ to our despairing world [*America*, April 21, 1984].

These insights of Henri Nouwen are clearly the fruit of a contemplative person giving himself up to the persons and world around him and taking the time to reflect deeply on these experiences. This same contemplative attitude can and should be directed toward the earth as well as toward humankind, and can also deepen the inner sense of solidarity. I experienced a glimpse of this truth during the first visit to Nicaragua and tried to share it in the following reflection:

Matagalpa

Beautiful Nicaragua—
your mountain breezes exchanging sun and clouds, warm
 and cool,
shimmering waters, sparkling ripples
against the greenest mountain backdrop—
everywhere green,
everything green.
I close my eyes to your sun, basking,
bathing, drinking deep your renewing rays,
matching the smiles of your people amused
by our lack of language in the bus,
smiles of sympathy too, simple smiles,
reaching out—solidarity.

Your mountains,
birthplace of your patriots,
calling your people
back to their roots,
rooting them in the promise of life—
sometimes rugged, stormy,
other times refreshing and stilling.
Today you still us,
uniting my spirit
with the spirit of your people—solidarity.

Solid mountains, still in place after centuries
of passings, the sweeping of skies
brushing your tops and moving on to the sea,
the swaying of your finger trees
reversing the ripples in your little lake
and reversing the rhythm of our days,
these lapping ripples flowing in front of my gaze,
softening, stilling—solidarity.

Solidarity,
unity of inner and outer, being and doing,
integrating, integral, full.

Pulling together,
gathering up the probing and pondering and running around,
weeks seeming like years,
yearning, wondering, watching, wishing, willing.

And your smells, wooded, fragrant.
Your sounds, buzzing, chirping,
ever blowing, rustling, rhythmic—
an ecstacy of sense.
Sensual mountains,
complete, filling out, fleshing out,
feeling the flow of these thought-filled days.
My muse, ever my muse,
moving, motivating,
the crown of Your glory,
O Creator of all,
All glory to You, forever,
but especially at this moment of Your movement of my heart.

FASTING

I feel hesitant and humbled in writing about something as interior as fasting, especially when I am so new to its possibilities and am so often being made aware of my weaknesses when I fast. But sharing our faith with one another is crucial, especially in "moments of supreme crisis," as the U.S. Catholic bishops in their pastoral letter on peace describe the present moment of human history.

Their call to fasting—as a means of reparation for our violence as individuals and collectively as a nation—is striking a responsive chord in many persons. The challenge that they issue, that God issues, that the world cries out for—namely, to take greater and greater risks for peace and justice—demands that we be both prophetic and prayerful. And I believe that we will be truly prophetic over the long haul only to the extent that we become more prayerful as we confront the destructiveness of U.S. policy in

Central America, as well as the evils of the nuclear arms race, and the callous disregard for the poor at home and abroad.

A Call to Prayer

Fast days should be special days of prayer, not just in periods set aside for prayerful reflection on the Scriptures but primarily in tiny moments throughout the day. In fasting from food, there are often many moments of wanting to eat during the day. These moments become opportunities and invitations to prayer—to speak with Jesus, to be more fully aware of his presence, to beg him for peace, to be reminded that God's will for the world truly is shalom. When our fast days are regular—at least weekly—this sense of prayerfulness seems to carry over to other days as well. Some combine their fast days with silence, to more consciously focus on the presence of God.

Different Forms of Fasting

Fasting takes many different forms—abstaining from all food and drink, skipping one or two meals or snacks, eliminating meat. But some persons cannot fast from food. They (and the rest of us) might consider other forms of fasting—fasting from television, from cigarettes, from liquor, from talking, from whatever it is that we overindulge in at times and that keeps us from being more single-minded about "seeking first the kingdom of God."

A Way of Expressing Our Dependence on God

The overwhelming sense of evil manifested in the arms race and suffering in Central America brings us to our knees, figuratively and literally. This sense of evil can drive us on to work harder for peace and justice, but it should also drive us back to God. After we have done what we can—writing Congress, giving talks, writing books or articles, mobilizing local groups, setting up "urgent action networks," vigiling and demonstrating, resisting war taxes, etc., etc.—we are faced with the realization that all that is still not enough. God, we depend on you. Raise up ever more courageous instruments of your peace. Work your miracles through others. Touch the hearts of decision-makers. Give courage to those victimized by the evils we are resisting. Give us greater courage, hope, and insight into your will and our role.

An Instrument of Discipleship

Jim Wallis in the November 1983 issue of *Sojourners* magazine reflects on the "cost of discipleship" and challenges us with Jesus' questions about whether we have "counted the cost" of following him (see Luke 14:25-33). Are we really willing to suffer or are we just "hanging around" the gospel? We are not sure how really willing we are to suffer for peace and justice, but we know that the tiny acts of self-denial involved in fasting can be a preparation for greater demands made by sacrificial love. Most of us do not jump from 0 to 10 in one leap. We move one step at a time. The pruning process (John 15:1-7) that God has in mind for each of us—calling us to be ever more willing to let go and follow Jesus—involves many moments of self-denial. Fasting can be an important part of this process, preparing us for the greater demands of sacrificial love.

A Means of Solidarity

A tiny no of self-denial can also be a tiny yes of solidarity. We can experience many moments of solidarity on fast days, as we bring to mind the lives of those victimized by the evils we are resisting—friends in Nicaragua, other victims of injustice we have met or read about, those persecuted for their convictions, peacemakers working hard for change. It might be especially helpful to write one such person each day we fast, to communicate that sense of solidarity and thus encourage them to remain faithful and strong. The more we bring to consciousness and prayer the lives of persons for whom or with whom we are resisting, the more deeply drawn into resistance and fidelity we are likely to find ourselves.

An Invitation to Service

The U.S. Catholic bishops recommend that fasting "be accompanied by works of charity and service toward our neighbors." Fast days are opportunities for fuller presence to those around us, if we do not allow our work schedule to dominate our day. Special little acts of service—doing an extra task for someone we live with, a phone call to a hurting friend or relative, time for a coworker at the office—make the solidarity of fasting more genuine. Those closest to us should also be the beneficiaries of our fasting.

Fasting and Prayer with Others

Another dimension of fasting and prayer is sharing them with other persons. Coming together regularly with several others for prayer and reflection on our resistance to injustice can be beneficial in several ways. Such sharing can broaden the insights that we arrive at in private reflection. Other persons sharing both our internal and external struggles can support us in difficult times, and challenge and inspire us to take the next, more risky, steps. Such sharing groups can also increase our level of awareness of issues and expand the outreach and thus the effectiveness of our solidarity actions, as well as help us persevere in this study and action, in our fasting and prayer, in our service and efforts at simplifying our lifestyles.

To be more serious about our solidarity projects and to sustain our prophetic efforts for justice and peace, we need to be engaged at the deepest levels of our being. Service, simplifying our lifestyle, prayer, and fasting all have a way of opening us up at these levels, making it possible for God to work more fully in our lives and in the world through us.

Resources

GROUPS/PROJECTS DESCRIBED IN THIS BOOK

American Friends Service Committee (1501 Cherry St., Philadelphia, PA 19102; 215-241-7000) directs a schools-supply project for Nicaragua and produces a variety of educational materials (see. chap. 7).

Bridgehead Trading (54 Jackman Av., Toronto, Ontario M4K 2X5; 416-463-0618) coordinates the Nicaraguan coffee project (and others) in Canada (see chap. 6).

Center for Defense Information (600 Maryland Ave. SW, Washington, DC 20024; 202-484-9490) produces policy analyses of U.S. foreign and military policy (see chap. 1).

Central America Peace Campaign (318 4th St. NE, Washington, DC 20017; 202-543-0873) is a coalition effort to promote an alternative U.S. policy for Central America and the Caribbean (see chap. 1 and 7).

Central American Historical Institute (Intercultural Center, Georgetown University, Washington, DC 20057) publishes *Envío* monthly for the U.S.A. in conjunction with the Instituto Histórico Centroamericano (Apartado A-194, Managua, Nicaragua).

Coalition for a New Foreign and Military Policy (712 "G" St. SE, Washington, DC 20003; 202-483-3391 is its Central American hot-line) produces periodical legislative updates on U.S. policy in Central America.

Friends of the Third World and **Cooperative Trading** (611 W. Wayne St., Ft. Wayne, IN 46802; 219-422-6821) is the U.S. coordinator of the Nicaraguan coffee project (and others) and related educational materials (see chap. 6).

158 RESOURCES

Institute for Peace and Justice (4144 Lindell Blvd., #400, St. Louis, MO 63108; 314-533-4445) coordinates the "Playgrounds, Not Battlegrounds" and other children's projects (see chap. 5) and pairing projects (see chap. 2 and 7).

MADRE (853 Broadway, Room 905, New York, NY 10003; 212-777-6470) is a friendship network with Nicaraguan groups offering pairing and other more personal solidarity projects as well as material aid projects (see chap. 7).

National Network in Solidarity with the People of Nicaragua and its **Humanitarian Aid for Nicaraguan Democracy** (HAND) relief project (2025 "I" St. NW, Washington, DC 20006; 202-223-2328) coordinates local Nicaraguan solidarity groups in the U.S.A. and work brigades to Nicaragua (see chap. 7).

Oxfam-America (115 Broadway, Boston, MA 02116; 617-482-1211) coordinates the "Tools for Peace" project (see chap. 7) and has produced short studies on its other Nicaraguan projects.

Policy Alternatives for the Caribbean and Central America (PACCA; c/o the Institute for Policy Studies, 1901 "Q" St. NW, Washington, DC 20009) is a coalition of U.S. groups promoting an alternative U.S. policy for Central America (see the "Central America Peace Campaign," above, and chap. 7).

Pueblo-to-People (5218 Chenevert, #5484, Houston, TX 77004; 713-523-1197) distributes Nicaraguan (and other Central American) handicrafts (see chap. 7).

Quixote Center (3311 Chauncey Place, #301, Mt. Rainier, MD 20712; 301-699-0042) coordinates the medical aid for Nicaragua project (see chap. 7) and produces a variety of short educational resources on Central America.

Witness for Justice and Peace (c/o SCM, Hart House, University of Toronto, Toronto, Ontario M5S 1A1) is the Canadian equivalent of the U.S. Witness for Peace effort; write or call Elly Kaas at 416-482-1613.

Witness for Peace (national office: P.O. Box 29241, Washington, DC 20017; 202-636-3642; see chap. 4, pp. 93-94 for regional addresses/phones) coordinates a nonviolent presence in Nicaragua and a direct action and public education campaign in the U.S.A.

AUDIOVISUAL AND PRINTED MATERIALS

The following bibliography is quite select, offering further resources primarily in relationship to the specific chapters/issues addressed in this book. For a more detailed bibliography, contact the National Network in Solidarity with the People of Nicaragua (above) or the North American Congress on Latin America (NACLA; see below).

Audiovisuals (describing specific projects in this book)

Amigos de los Niños (1984) is a 12-minute, 70-frame slide/tape presentation on the children of Nicaragua, on how North American children can respond to their situation, and on the "Playgrounds, Not Battlegrounds" project in particular. From the Institute for Peace and Justice. Purchase, $48; $20 rental.

Media Network (288 W. 13th St., New York, NY 10011) publishes a comprehensive guide to films on Central America including information on ordering, a guide to equipment, a list of distributors, descriptions and reviews of films, and tips on how to use them effectively; $2.50. Icarus Films (200 Park Av. South, New York, NY 10003) has a Central America film library that includes such films on Nicaragua as *Thank God and the Revolution, Sandino, Today and Forever, Dawn of the People: The Nicaraguan Literacy Crusade.*

Nicaragua: Where Everybody's Learning (1983) is a 15-minute slide/tape presentation from the American Friends Service Committee (above) recounting the personal experience of a school teacher who worked in Nicaragua and the school supplies project (see chap. 5). Purchase, $25; rental $10.

Paraíso is a 30-minute film from Maryknoll Films (Maryknoll, NY 10545) describing Fr. Miguel d'Escoto's community of Fundeci in León in the mid-1970s (where some of the playgrounds are now being built—see chap. 7); excellent for a view of Nicaragua before 1979 from both the perspectives of the wealthy and the poor, and for a view of what poverty can do to a people.

Patria Libre o Morir (1982) is a 20-minute 120-frame slide/tape presentation describing the Nicaraguan model of development and specific ways to support peace and justice for Nicaragua, including pairing projects;

from the Institute for Peace and Justice. Purchase, $65; rental, $20. Individual slides of Nicaraguan pairing groups are also available.

Peace for Two Peoples (1984) is a 15-minute, 80-frame slide/tape presentation on life in Nicaragua in the midst of war, on Witness for Peace, and how North Americans can promote peace and justice for Nicaragua. From the Institute for Peace and Justice. Purchase, $60; rental, $20.

World Hunger: The Cost of Coffee (1980) is a 15-minute filmstrip telling the story of coffee—the workers, the colonial patterns and mechanisms governing the production/distribution of coffee, and how North Americans can relate to these realities. Purchase from Franciscan Communications (1229 S. Santee, Los Angeles, CA 90015) for $38; rental from Visions (506 E. Yandell, El Paso, TX 79902) for the cost of postage only.

Books

Berryman, Phillip. *What's Wrong in Central America and What to Do about It* (American Friends Service Committee, 1984). Excellent 60-page analysis of U.S. policy in Central America; the section on Nicaragua is summarized in the August 1984 issue of *Sojourners*.

Cabestrero, Teófilo. *Ministers of God, Ministers of the People: Testimonies of Faith from Nicaragua* (1983, Orbis Books, Maryknoll, NY 10545; ZED Press, 57 Caledonian Rd., London N19DN). In-depth interviews with three Catholic priests in the Nicaraguan Revolutionary government: Ernesto Cardenal, minister of culture; Miguel d'Escoto, foreign minister; Fernando Cardenal, national vice-coordinator of the Sandinista Youth Movement.

Collins, Joseph. *What Difference Could a Revolution Make? Food and Farming in the New Nicaragua* (1982, Institute for Food and Development Policy, 1885 Mission St., San Francisco, CA 94103). The best study of Nicaraguan agricultural policy available, with a personal dimension as well.

Lappé, Frances Moore. *Now We Can Speak: A Journey through the New Nicaragua* (Institute for Food and Development Policy, 1982). Brings the various dimensions of the new Nicaragua alive through interviews with a variety of Nicaraguans creating a new society.

McGinnis, James. *Educating for Peace and Justice: Global Dimensions* (Institute for Peace and Justice, 1985 edition). Includes a special case study for high-school and college teachers on the Nicaraguan Revolution.

Randall, Margaret. *Sandino's Daughters* (1981, New Star Books, Vancouver and Toronto; Crossing Press, Trumansburg, NY 14886). The role of women in the Nicaraguan Revolution, many of whom hold key positions in the Nicaraguan government today.

Rosset, Peter, and John Vandermeer, eds. *The Nicaraguan Reader: Documents of a Revolution under Fire* (Grove Press, 1983). A comprehensive collection of articles, essays, and policy statements by U.S. and Nicaraguan officials and observers, with sections on "the Nicaraguan threat" and U.S. intervention, as well as various dimensions of life in the new Nicaragua.

Periodicals and Pamphlets

Envío. A monthly in-depth analysis of current events and issues in Nicaragua edited by an international team of analysts at the Instituto Histórico Centroamericano (see above). At $25/year, it is the best resource for regular updating on Nicaragua.

Land and Hunger: Nicaragua (1983). A 6-page background paper from Bread for the World (802 Rhode Island Ave. NE, Washington, DC 20018). Provides a view of the Nicaraguan Revolution through its land and agricultural policies: 20¢ each; $15/100.

Literacy Crusade in Nicaragua: A Report. Focus of the *Bulletin* (vol. 12, no. 2, 1981) of the Council on Interracial Books for Children (1841 Broadway, New York, NY 10023). Provides both personal accounts of young *brigadistas* and analysis of the literacy campaign as a whole.

NACLA Report on the Americas. Has carried features on Nicaragua, including "Nicaragua's Revolution," May-June 1980 (NACLA, 151 W. 19th St., New York, NY 10011).

Sojourners (P.O. Box 29272, Washington, DC 20017). The March 1983 issue is devoted entirely to Nicaragua. Presents personal reflection/accounts by Nicaraguan leaders and good articles on church-state tensions and the Miskito Amerindians issue.

Talking Sense about Nicaragua. A 14-page pamphlet from the American Friends Service Committee (above), providing an overall assessment of the Nicaraguan Revolution, current controversies, and U.S. policy: 25¢ each; $15/100.

The Truth about Nicaragua (1984), from the Quixote Center (Box 5206, Hyattsville, MD 20782). An 8-page tabloid summarizing many of the key issues—the Miskito Amerindians, the church, the economy, the war. An excellent overview.

The World in your Coffee Cup. A 36-page booklet published jointly by the Campaign Co-op (35 Cowley Rd., Oxford, England) and the World Development Movement (Bedford Chambers, Covent Garden, London WC2E 8HA).